GET UP
Girl

God, Jesus, and **The Holy Spirit** in my
Midst, my Middle, and my Margins

SALLY TAYLOR

CLAY BRIDGES

Get Up Girl
God, Jesus, and The Holy Spirit in my Midst, my Middle, and my Margins
Copyright © 2025 by Sally Taylor

Published by Clay Bridges Press in Houston, TX
www.ClayBridgesPress.com

eISBN: 978-1-68488-136-9
ISBN: 978-1-68488-135-2

Special Sales: Most Clay Bridges titles are available in special quantity discounts. Custom imprinting or excerpting can also be done to fit special needs. Contact Clay Bridges at Info@ClayBridgesPress.com

Dedicated to the Ones who think that they are too broken for The Lord to redeem.

Table of Contents

Preface   v

Chapter 1: The Broken Road   1

Chapter 2: Is This a Pothole or a Sinkhole?   9

Chapter 3: Bliss, Babies, and the Birth of Heart Worship   23

Chapter 4: Family, Firsts, and Fields of Dreams   35

Chapter 5: Failures, Gifts, and Holy Kinship   45

Chapter 6: Coworkers, Conviction, Damsels, and
Destruction   57

Chapter 7: And Even the Saints Didn't See This Coming   65

Chapter 8: 1999—The Year of the Interloper   75

Chapter 9: The Prowler That Remained   87

Chapter 10: Running Headlong into Insanity   101

Chapter 11: Mirror, Mirror on the Wall   111

Chapter 12: Messages, Meditations, and Margins   129

Chapter 13: It's All About Perspective   141

Chapter 14: Finding My Purpose and Walking in
My ECHO   153

Chapter 15: The Helper That Fellowships, Frees, and Heals   171

Chapter 16: Using Your Failures, Faith, Fellowship,
and Even Your Face for Ministry   189

In Closing   203

Special Thanks   209

Preface

This is my very real story told in very real language, mixed with God's Word along with how He has spoken into my life along the way. I want you to feel like we are having coffee at my kitchen table. I had a kindred sister in Christ who reminded me that our perspective is a huge part of how we receive things. I told her my testimony was ugly but full of God's presence. She said it might be an ugly story, but it is beautiful because God is all over it.

Hang on tight as I tell my story. It's gonna be a wild ride, but with the right perspective, I believe you will hear God speak. Prepare yourself for the ups and the downs mixed with storms that end in victories, washed in the Lord's mercy, followed by flashes of miracles. Hang in there to the end and bask in the love. See how my journey is a testimony bathed in peace.

Dearest Father God, I want you to shine in me and my story, for it is not a testimony of only sadness and brokenness but of victory in and through You. I pray my words and my story elevate You. It shows what a constant You have been in my entire life. And despite my stubbornness, arrogance, and rebellious judgment, You have loved me unconditionally without reserve or regard for my failures. Father, You are my stronghold. There is nothing stronger than You in my life, and to You be all the glory. May You always be in my midst, my middle, and my margins.

"May the words of my mouth and the meditation of my heart be pleasing to you, O LORD, my rock and my redeemer" (Psalm 19:14 NLT).

In Jesus's name, Amen.

Chapter 1
The Broken Road

I'm not one of those people whose childhood memories begin in infancy. My earliest memory came much later. But the Lord remembers me from my earliest beginnings.

> Psalm 139:13-16 says, *"For you created my innermost being; you knit me together in my mother's womb. I praise you because I am fearfully and wonderfully made; your works are wonderful; I know that full well. My frame was not hidden from you when I was made in the secret place, when I was woven together in the depths of the earth your eyes saw my unformed body. All the days ordained for me were written in your book before one of them came to be."*

My mother, bless her heart, had two daughters and three or four miscarriages before I was born. But I survived her hostile womb, and at the age of 42, she gave birth to me, a third girl, and my brother came along one year later. I can't even imagine that. I learned later in life that my father didn't believe I was his. He even refused to provide for me or replace any baby stuff that was long gone because I was not expected to be, and my older sisters were ages six and eight when I was born. Fortunately, my mother had friends at work and at church who sowed into my little life with all I needed to get started.

In knowing the story of Christ dying on the cross, I know that Jesus knows how it is and how much it hurts for your father to look away from you in your time of need. I don't remember my earliest years, but my mother told me I was always independent. I shied away from any kind of cuddling, even during the scariest of thunderstorms. I'm not sure if I was like that because of nature or nurture. I think my earliest memory was when I was six years old. I remember lying in what we used to call a station wagon. These days, we have SUVs. I was in a grocery store parking lot feeling horrible. My stomach hurt so badly that I began to throw up. I was terrified that I would be in trouble because I had made a mess. As it turned out, my appendix was on the verge of bursting. I was taken to the hospital after my mom discovered what had happened in her absence, and I was rushed into surgery. I don't remember much of my hospital stay or my recovery. Looking back, I guess it was an example of what would turn out to be one of the Lord's many protections over my young life.

Some of my sweetest memories are from my earliest friendship with my friend Sandy. She was into all the childhood shenanigans with me. We climbed up into a tree house and fought off the neighborhood boys using charcoal briquettes from the barbecue grill. We also bounced on what I believe may have been one of the first outdoor bouncy toys for kids. It was nothing more than a tire inner tube from a giant construction vehicle. We bounced on that thing for hours. Sandy also thought it would be fun to get inside a discarded refrigerator box with me and roll down our neighbor's hill, right toward the road. I can think of so many reasons why all this was dangerous, but God watched out for Sandy and me.

One morning when Sandy and I were kicking around a ball, I chased after it across the street. As I was making my way back, a panel van came around the corner at full speed and hit me. Sandy would tell you still to this day that she saw my leg go under the front tire. That accident would be the first of many that would have, could have, or should have taken my life, if God's hand wasn't upon me.

During all these adventures with Sandy, not once did she or anybody else ever spend the night at my house because my father was a terrible alcoholic. I think the hardest thing about having an alcoholic dad was the lack of normalcy in my life. Not only did I never have sleepovers, but I was always terrified that he would act out in front of my friends. The drinking was constant until his health started to fail. I watched him have a heart attack and prayed I wouldn't have to give him CPR. I could positively say that I didn't like my dad, and I'm pretty sure I borderline hated him at that time. But I held out hope that one day I might love him just like Sandy loved her daddy. I was always looking to be loved by my earthly father. But my search for validation, importance, and love continued to no avail.

How true it is that you never know what goes on behind closed doors. In my childhood home, that was more than true. My dad set the tone for almost everything in our home. In most homes, especially a Christian home, the father is the leader, the protector, and the provider. My dad was the influencer. He affected the atmosphere and could influence everything we experienced when he was there.

In John 14:18, Jesus tells us He will never leave us as orphans, but He will come to us. Scripture also says we are to receive the kingdom like an innocent, helpless child who can't obtain it on their own. No matter how much I tried, I wasn't able to convince anyone to welcome me into the special place of their heart. But at that time, I didn't recognize my position in God's heart and His protection and provisions for my life. It would be much later that I would learn just how special I was to God.

In relation to my earthly father, I was always fearful of my dad's behavior when he was drinking. I yearned for peace or normalcy. I wanted that so desperately that I would have done anything to fix whatever problem there was in our home, just to keep the peace. Eventually, I reasoned that if I was the best I could be, things would be easier for my mom. She would at least have one less life whose happiness she thought she had total responsibility for.

My mom once told me I was mature, independent, and smart. I guess I was doing all right under the circumstances, but I realized later that I had what is now called codependency, and so did my mother. And just like my mom, I got my validation and found importance trying to make everything right. I reasoned that if I could help my mom fix things, she might be happy. That was a lot for a little girl to feel responsible for.

I also ended up trying to take care of myself as much as I could, thinking I was taking responsibility for me off her to-do list. She spent time trying to keep my dad happy but also a lot of time trying to make sure my younger brother, and my oldest sister were headed in the right direction. Apparently, she thought they needed more of that than I did. If it hadn't been for my sister Libby who was six years older, I would have had no one making sure I was headed in the right direction. I would have felt all alone in that house if it hadn't been for her. I really looked up to Libby. She was and still is very much like me in the independence department. She also did what she had to do to get by. She took great care of me, understood how I felt, and kept me safe until she found a way out of our scenario. At 16, she was hardly on our mom's radar. And our dad's participation in our family was just to remind us of who the boss was.

My sister dug her way out of our dysfunction right into her own through a teenage marriage with motherhood right on the horizon. But she tried the best she could to still take care of me when she had time. I think we clung to each other so closely because we understood each other and saw life through the same eyes of a yearning to matter. One description of a sister is a kindred. She and I are kindred spirits. We found a belonging with each other because we experienced life with similar deficits. We were both looking for a tribe—a family to belong to. She left and created her own, and I continued to look for my belonging among friends and their families. The longest cycle of my life began when Libby left.

I understand the lack of connection with my dad, but I would have given anything to feel special to my mom, and not just because I was easy. Like me, she didn't have any friends over to the house. I was as close to a friend as she would get. Some mothers and daughters can be best friends, but with us, it was a burden I was not able to handle. Being mother's friend and confidant was not what a little kid, especially a preteen needed. I wanted to be a loved and cherished daughter.

Some of the things mom shared with me did a lot to define who I thought I was. I don't understand her reasons for telling me the things she did that broke my heart and my spirit. For example, she always gave my brother special treatment, and her explanation was that he is the only boy and doesn't have a father. Well, Mom, regarding having a normal father, none of us kids had one. But those words made me even more determined to make sure to be strong for myself because who else was going to?

Some who knew my mother would never believe she was anything short of perfect because she was sweet, loving, creative, strong, and so much of what I wanted to be. Years later, I had a light bulb moment and had to give my mom some grace because she was doing the best she could with what she had to deal with. Let there be no mistake, neither Mom nor I were perfect, but I am so thankful that she gave me the legacy of knowing God and Jesus. I just wish I had grasped that before I entered my teenage years.

Chapter 2

Is This a Pothole or a Sinkhole?

Whoever remains stiff-necked after many rebukes will suddenly be destroyed— without a remedy.

—Proverbs 29:1

In the years to come, I pushed the limits on what would constitute being stiff-necked. I continued to have no limits to what I would do to have half a chance for the love I was looking for. Some of it was even innocent.

Sandy and I continued to be close into our preteen and teenage years. I spent a lot of time at her house and with her family. Her parents treated me just like one of their own, especially if I needed to have an attitude adjustment or some direction meant to keep me safe. I discovered that during my preteen years I was searching for the love of a family.

Sandy and I had friends on the same street. They were sisters named June and Sheila Casey. They participated in most of our misadventures. It's a wonder any of us lived to tell of our childhood. June and Sheila's parents and most all the parents in our neighborhood helped raise me and keep me safe. The Caseys sold their house and moved away. Sandy and I initially thought it was the worst thing ever, but we were wrong. When June and Sheila moved, our parents took us to see the Caseys at their new house. It seemed so far, but it was probably less than two miles away. We met June and Sheila's new friend. Her name was Terri, and immediately she became a favorite to Sandy and me. Terri lived with her dad because her parents were divorced. Her dad was bigger than life and a gentle giant. He also signed on to keep an eye on my well-being.

I hate to think what would have happened to me if I had not had so many wonderful adults who cared about me the way they all did. I continued to broaden my geographical horizons in my friendships. That is so funny considering my destinations were mostly just blocks from my house.

Sandy and I met another Sandy a couple streets away, and we all hung out together as we moved into our teens. There were also new neighbors—the Bateys—behind my house, and I spent time there as well. Ma and Pa Batey, as I called them, also watched after me. But as much as I loved them, my best normal family experiences around a kitchen table were with my new friend, Julie Whitson. I remember spending hours around that table with her parents and one of her younger brothers.

Those were the days that people smoked in their homes, so I always remember cigarette smoke in the air and country music on the radio. Julie's dad was a bit gruff but not mean. I guess that felt somewhat familiar, but her mom was a direct contrast to mine. She was strong in a different way—confident. My mom was strong, but she let people walk all over her. Not Becky Whitson. She was someone you knew would set you straight if you needed it. She would also kiss you on top of your head before you went to bed during a sleepover. I knew she loved her kids and me. I learned a balance of strength, discipline, and love from Miss Becky.

In my search to be special to someone, I learned tactics to insinuate myself in people's lives. After a while, I couldn't tell if my tactics had opened doors or if I was appreciated for who I really was. I had no confidence in either. As with all teenage girls, thinking about boys was very natural. With me it was a lot deeper. I had started looking for the one who could fix all that was wrong in my home and my heart. I wanted to be special to someone. As I look back at how I was back then, I think I probably had "desperate" written all over me. Like an animal can sense fear, a different kind of animal, a teenage boy, can sense desperation. He will either run from the drama, and that is a good thing, or he may use it to his advantage as a bargaining chip to get what he wants. Either way, raging hormones in teens wreak havoc in the insecure searching of a teenage female or teenage male. With me, that was a whole other bucket of dysfunction.

I experienced young love and had my first boyfriend in the summer of the eighth grade. I remember taking him to a family reunion at my grandmother's house. It was so obvious that our being left alone spelled trouble. Because of that, all my older cousins had to take a shift chaperoning us for the weekend. After that short-lived relationship, the next two years became like a job for me, and my task was to find love. But I never completed my task. No matter how short the short-shorts were or how tight the jeans, I was uselessly searching to be loved and feel special. But the next season of my life would change my life forever. Believe it or not, I would call this the favorite time of my life.

When I started high school, there was a new crop of candidates from other schools to give my heart to. They didn't know my story, so I made myself over. Instead of being obnoxious and desperate, I switched gears to become sweet, quiet, and mysterious. I came with a ready-made set of friends. The girls from the other schools were like a larger group of the "Pink Ladies" from Grease, and my group was like Sandy, or "Sandra Dee," from the movie. In the middle of the storm of hormones, everyone was trying to find themselves. I was struggling with that because the person I thought I was, was not at all who I was trying to be.

Most teens drift away from church during their high school years. My mom was struggling to keep me in church. I wish I had noticed that it was in church that I was truly loved and cared for, and that I was able to be my authentic self. I was naturally witty and funny just like my mom. We were both super creative, and my mom made me participate in every mother-daughter sketch that she wrote. I would ham it up and be over-the-top silly, and everyone loved it. I was the direct opposite of quiet, and I was not mysterious. I was out there, and I didn't care. But I would go back to school and fall back into my created facade. It was within that created persona, I thought I would fit.

It was at the end of the 10th grade that I think I bumped my head and completely lost my mind when I thought I met the love of my life. His name was Scott. He was different. He was just as mysterious and moody as my created persona. He was also from a different high school on the other side of town. He started coming to my school when he moved in with his dad who lived in my school district. I can't remember how it happened, but from the moment we met, we were inseparable. I felt a kindred spirit with him like I hadn't felt since my older sister. But looking back, I now see it was because he was carrying around the same baggage full of family dysfunction as I was. He understood me because, like my sister, he saw life through the same eyes of hurt, disappointment, loss, and insecurity.

When I met Scott, I was a flirt, but I was relatively innocent. Everything I had in my arsenal to get attention was unnecessary. Scott was happy to be the object of my adoration, and I was thrilled to be his. He brought an air of sophistication that was in total contrast to my world. He had money, a fast car, and a confidence that came from his life on the other side of town. His stepfather was a prominent lawyer in Charlotte, North Carolina, and he had a mother who worshiped him. But Scott was a little wild, and that might have been why he was sent to live with his father. Scott may have viewed where he lived as the wrong side of the tracks.

I was mesmerized by Scott, and I couldn't imagine my life without him. I began to do whatever I had to do so that would never be my reality. I lost my virginity to Scott. I was sure he was the one who deserved to be the one I would give it to. That started years of using intimacy to make myself feel special. But the very thing that I thought made me special to Scott was the very thing I began to use to hold onto him. All the things that had bonded us together before took a back seat to our physical relationship.

Scott was a year ahead of me in school. When he graduated, he moved on to be a working man. He even left his dad's house and moved across town to live in a house with four other guys. The house was an older craftsman home that could have been very beautiful if it had not been inhabited by five young bachelors. Since he was living on his own, we had even more chances to be alone. Scott also sparked a scheming heart in me.

I began to tell my mother lies about spending the weekend with friends I knew from my part-time job. Being without Scott at school was very hard, and I began to skip morning classes to meet Scott at his house before he went to work. I still loved high school, and I still had my core friend group. I was also in my second year of being the manager of the football team. I was very smart when it came to schoolwork. I was in several exclusive clubs that you had to qualify for, including the National Honor Society, and I knew I wanted to go to college. But as much as I loved all this, there were times I just didn't show up because I was distracted by my obsession with Scott. I lost myself in that relationship. I was very smart in school, but I was stupid in what would prove to be just an imitation of the love I was looking for.

I received several invitations to attend the universities I applied to. The coach of my high school football team stuck his neck out for me and helped me with my application to Georgia Tech to study sports medicine. That turned into an offer for a full-ride scholarship. Georgia Tech and other invitations would have opened doors to a possible full and successful life for me, but I couldn't look farther down the road than the current moment to believe I could be a success without Scott. I turned down the full-ride scholarship and took an offer at the University of North Carolina at Charlotte so I would be able to hold onto Scott.

My senior year of high school progressed into the year I would be forced to grow up. In the fall, I began to feel very sick. I had never been a sickly kid. I thought I had my first case of the flu, but with the teasing of a few of my girlfriends, I secretly took a pregnancy test. I was naively shocked to find out I was pregnant. I told one of my closest friends who I knew wouldn't judge me because I was keeping some big secrets of hers.

I can't remember why I told another friend, but she volunteered to go with me to get the abortion Scott paid for. Scott couldn't figure out how to take time off work to support me through the worst day of my life. After that day, life went back to normal for everyone but me. I didn't talk about it, but I was so devastated that I thought my heart would surely collapse. Scott and I still saw each other, but we were never the same. We broke up after I graduated. We didn't seem to have too much in common anymore. And I did go to college.

I found out years later that Scott had kept tabs on me as my life moved on. He knew about all my milestones. I also found out that he had two daughters and had named the first one after me. I also discovered that he could tell me exactly how old that child would be whose life we had ended—with that awful choice that so many scared teenagers make.

The year that followed was horrible, but it showed that God was still faithful to keep me safe. He was still watching over this teenage girl who chose to walk away from Him and the Lutheran church. I was almost soaked in my sadness and regret. I had this secret that would one day escape and be more than I could handle. One suicide attempt and hospitalization would be followed by a second attempt in which I was determined to end the pain once and for all. I picked the largest oak tree near my house to drive my mom's car into at full speed, totaling the car. But I walked away with only a broken nose and bruised ribs. God had other plans for me. I wish I had recognized the all-encompassing love it took for God to not walk away from this deceitful, broken young woman.

I'm not sure if you could call this irony or God's plan, but my major at UNC-Charlotte was psychology. I was very good at it, and I thought I had found my path. My thesis would be published in the school's psychological journal. Shortly after that, I was forced to slow down this potential path and ultimately quit school after my dad had a heart attack and I had to quit work for a while. I had to help my family financially, so I got a full-time job. Resentment bubbled within me like a molten lava flow.

My high school connections were still tight and remain close even to this day. People I knew in high school were on their college journeys or got grown-up jobs. Our circle expanded to include other people who happened to have the same grown-up jobs. As our friendships formed, social occasions were mixed with new faces.

In October of 1981, I was invited to a Halloween party that some of my friends were going to. It was just the place to bury my brokenness in my new habit of noise and alcohol. But it just so happened that I met one of the new faces there who was now in the mix. His name was Geofrey. We hit it off as much as you can in a blind stupor. We exchanged phone numbers and as time passed, began to get to know each other. We were very different. He was from across the county and lived in what was back then a rural part of Charlotte. Even though I talked about disco dances, and he talked about tractor pulls, we were smitten with each other.

More and more we ended up at the same neighborhood watering hole near my house. That soon progressed to attending the softball games that he and some of the guys I knew from school played in. I was not the only female groupie at these games, and a whole new set of girlfriends bloomed in my world. The only way I can describe what happened next is to call it assumptions and automatic pairing. Couples were established, and we ran in a pack. There were about four to six couples who did almost everything together. As some vowed love and devotion to each other, others split and then came back together over and over. Conversations between couples who had been together since high school began to evolve into plans for the future.

The seriousness happened between the immature craziness of group beach trips. Obviously, on these beach trips there were no moral boundaries for any of us, and we were acting as if our futures were already bound by marriage. But I made sure I would never have to make another life-derailing decision again. Lust began to build futures based on delusions of forever after. One after another, I wore many a blissful smile and ugly bridesmaid dress. I knew that what I witnessed was exactly what I also wanted. Soon the talk of a future was mine to have. We followed the pack in the same direction, and the Christmas of 1983, I got the ring. I was finally headed in the normal that I had for so many years yearned for.

I will never forget the day he told his mother and sister that we were getting married. I'm not sure if the sister knew I was in the next room and could hear the whole conversation or if she even cared, but it was clear that she thought I was beneath him and his family. Those sentiments about me lingered far beyond that moment. Our wedding took a year to plan. Neither of us were from families with the means to pay for a large wedding. My mother made all the bridesmaid dresses out of a sapphire blue taffeta material. The cake had the same color blue flowers trailing down it. The reception was put together by all the little ladies of my Lutheran church. We had beautiful tea sandwiches, and nuts and mints. It was just as I had imagined.

Traditionally, the Lutheran church is very ceremonial in all it does. We spoke the words of the marriage ceremony in the Lutheran book of worship. I was elated when it all came together on November 10, 1984, and we were pronounced husband and wife. Now I could begin to build a family that I had high hopes for. We greeted our guests and hugged our relatives and friends. But after all the ordinary wedding pictures were taken, I began to look for my new husband who had gone missing. He had gone back into the sanctuary. With him was his mother, his two sisters, and their families. I happily entered the sanctuary and came bounding up the aisle and asked, "What ya doing back in here?" I didn't expect what I heard next.

My new husband told me to go back to the reception hall, and he would be there after they finished taking family pictures. Wait a minute. I thought I was part of this family now. I turned and left with the deafening sound of my bubble bursting in my ear. Innocent or not, it was hurtful. At that moment, on that day, I believe a definite tone was set for our entire marriage. The Lord ordained the plan for marriage when He made Eve from Adam's rib.

> *Genesis 2:22-24 says, "Then the Lord God made a woman from the rib he had taken out of the man, and he brought her to the man. The man said, 'This is now bone of my bones and flesh of my flesh; she shall be called 'woman,' for she was taken out of man.' That is why a man leaves his father and mother and is united to his wife, and they become one flesh."*

I didn't feel like that happened that day. I was crushed. I am sure that if the design God had for marriage was the prototype for us, our marriage would have turned out differently. I married so many people that day and so many opinions. But there were only two of us paying the bills and having the arguments about those many opinions.

We continued to be part of our large social circle of friends. The guys still had softball, and they added golf and coaching Pop Warner football. We even lived in the same rental community of duplexes as half the crew. Luckily—no, let me rephrase that—by the grace of God, my husband's best friend had married a girl from Kansas where he went to college. Her name was Dana. Oh, sweet Dana was so peaceful, quiet, and loving. She became my best friend. She would be the level-headed, calming voice to me with my still broken spirit. She was a devoted wife, and I admired her in so many ways. She and her husband seemed to be the envy of more than just me. She had a strong faith that probably kept her so calm. I wanted and needed that. I longed for the reason for Dana's peace. Church for me had been flannel board Bible stories, and my only prayers were still said from the words in a book or printed in a bulletin and recited corporately. I felt like I needed more, and I didn't yet know if it was in my marriage or in my faith—or both.

Chapter 3

Bliss, Babies, and the Birth of Heart Worship

O ur first wedding anniversary was shared with the Pop Warner football city championships. We did celebrate and never looked any deeper into what could improve our marriage. We did the next thing we thought it was time for, and six weeks later, after three pregnancy tests, we acknowledged that we were about to open our next chapter because I was pregnant.

I loved being pregnant. I was sick only one day, and that could have just been something I ate. Nothing changed for the hubby. There was still softball, golf, and hanging out with the guys in our neighborhood. I was thankful that there were other wives for me to hang out with. Our topics of discussion centered around decorating our homes, fashion, what the future might hold, and of course complaining about our husbands. We all agreed it was only when they showed up for mealtime that we had a chance to share our hopes and dreams. I could imagine that they would in turn have a laugh with their buds about what we thought was important.

There's an ironic fact that I failed to mention when I was describing the neighborhood. The giant 100-year-old oak tree that I drove my mom's car into on one of my suicide attempts was behind our duplex. I could see it from the back porch. And better yet, it was right in front of Dana's duplex. It seems to me that God is in the habit of connecting my life events, and they remind me how blessed I am and how He has delivered me time after time. They appear like lighted steppingstones, not necessarily as stumbling blocks. But that is a revelation that has come as hindsight. I was clueless of that at the time. I had not yet started to recognize the presence of God in my life because my relationship with Him at that time was in a book or a bulletin and nothing more. But the verses from a psalm were still true for me.

Psalm 139:11-13,15-16 says, "If I say, 'Surely the darkness will hide me and the light become night around me,' even the darkness will not be dark to you; the night will shine like the day for darkness is as light to you. For you created my inmost being; you knit me together in my mother's womb. My frame was not hidden from you when I was made in the secret place, when I was woven together in the depths of the earth. Your eyes saw my unformed body; all the days ordained for me were written in your book before one of them came to be."

Again, this is hindsight, and the reason I didn't include verse 14 was because I had not yet learned to praise God, and I had no idea how much praise I owed Him.

Pregnancy hormones are no joke, and they are vicious sometimes. I would be deliriously happy one minute and crying like a waterfall the next. Bless Dana and all the other girls for putting up with me. I believe it was around this time that Dana and I began to work together. That was fun, and she was my closest relationship at work and at home.

On one of my sad, frustrated, lonely nights, I walked to her duplex. I was very pregnant and, in my pajamas, as I walked down the road. She consoled me as she always did, but this night she took charge on my behalf. She got on the phone and called the neighborhood testosterone cave and reminded my husband that his wife was pregnant and there with her, but I needed to be with him more. She was so stern and authoritative that she gave him no options. That would prove to be only the first time Dana would step in to help me.

We all know that arguments and relationship struggles are almost never the fault of only one person. I was still the same broken spirit I was back in my childhood and teenage years. And on top of that, I was fiercely protective of the times I felt part of a family of two and soon to be three. I have to admit that I was jealous of how much time my husband chose to spend with his friends. I wanted to be his only focus, and that wasn't fair or possible all the time. But I did want to be what he sought out to find happiness at least sometimes.

I seemed to sabotage my own wants and needs by being a fussy, complaining, hateful woman. I could say that all of this could be blamed on pregnancy, but that would be a lie. I was growing into the last person my husband wanted to hang out with. Instead of becoming the person in the prayer that says, "Lord, please show me how to become the person that the person I want to marry wants to marry." I was anything but that. I had put pressure on him to fill all the cracks in my broken spirit and heal the giant hole in my heart that remained. I didn't have a clue that he was never made to do any of that. There was something missing in my life, but I hoped it would be filled by the little person who was growing inside me. I was sure that being a mother and having a family would finally make me whole.

There seemed to be an unspoken pattern that we were trying to follow that was being established by our circle of friends. The next thing on the agenda was home ownership. On January 28, 1986, we put a bid on a three-bedroom, one-bath house that happened to be in the neighborhood I would have given anything to live in when I was a teenager. All the cool kids lived there. I was finally gonna be cool, and maybe even accepted. Ninety days later, we were homeowners. When I was five months pregnant, we moved in. We burned the midnight oil painting, organizing, planning, and putting together a nursery for our new little one who would come soon. As I mentioned before, I loved being pregnant and having a constant companion. Everything was going very smoothly. I was getting huge. In the end, I would only gain 27 pounds.

Five weeks before my due date, we expanded our family by adding a cute little Beagle puppy to the mix, and Wylie came to live with us. He was named for my mother's side of the family. I adored him, and he adored me. One month before our baby was born, we found out that I had a major blood pressure issue. I would have to leave work early and be on bed rest at home for the rest of my pregnancy.

My high blood pressure continued, and I was admitted to the hospital for supervised bed rest for a week. I was told

I would be induced into labor and delivery. I had gotten so big that I could not even touch my fingertips together around my huge belly. The day came for me to be induced, and I was moved to a labor and delivery room. I was hooked up to an IV of Pitocin, which was used to start my contractions and with no results that first day, they started this process again in the morning for two more days, It was exhausting, so my husband went home at night, only to come back the next morning and start this all over again.

By the third day with no progress toward delivery, my husband decided to go home and try to get some sleep and then go back to work. When he was about to leave for work that night, he got the call that my water had finally broken, and I was now in natural labor. I guess God and this baby decided they would not be rushed. The funny thing is that this would be the temperament of this child.

I was put in a recovery room instead of labor and delivery because none of those rooms were available. It was a busy night. They parked me in this little curtain-draped area, and my water broke again. This time it flooded the bed and rained onto the floor. If I remember right, my husband got back to the hospital just as they got me into a real labor and delivery room. It was a new trend back then that women would try to deliver their babies naturally with no pain killers. I lasted with that until I was 6 centimeters dilated, and then I asked for an epidural. The epidural was a challenge to say the least because of how big my belly was. But it was in, and I waited for the pain to ease off. It felt about the same but was bearable.

Then an attending doctor came in to check my progress and discovered that the baby had a bowel movement and was in distress. It was now necessary for me to have an emergency C- section. I was wheeled into the operating room. My husband joined me, standing by my head all decked out in scrubs and a mask. I had absolutely no knowledge that the epidural should have stopped my pain if it was inserted correctly, but I was sure I wasn't supposed to feel them cut into my belly. I yelled out that I could feel that. They stopped and said there's no way that was possible. I said I did feel it and said, "Watch this," and I lifted my legs. There was a lot of fast and furious activity all around me. They said they would give me something for the pain in my IV but that they couldn't stop.

Back in those days, the overhead lights were covered in chrome, and I could look up and see them take out all my organs that were in the way and put them up on my chest. What they did to deliver my baby, IV or not, felt like they were pulling my back muscles out the front. It was completely horrible until I heard the cry of my beautiful baby and heard the words, "It's a girl." At that moment it felt like all was well with the world because I was now a mommy to Melissa Nicole. She would change my life forever in so many ways.

Mark 9:37 says, "Whoever welcomes one of these little children in my name welcomes me; and whoever welcomes me does not welcome me but the one who sent me." Looking back, I realize that Melissa's birth changed more than just the size of our family; it changed the way I looked at a lot of things. I had been taught who God and Jesus are and knew a few basic stories, but I believe it was now that I began to yearn for more of a relationship with Jesus. I now had a responsibility to teach my child about Jesus. It's been said, "You can't teach what you don't know." Melissa was and still is beautiful. She weighed 9 pounds, 9 ounces at her birth, and I couldn't keep my eyes off her. One of my favorite times of the day was late at night or in the wee hours of the morning when I had her all to myself at feeding time. It was hard to share her with anybody else after having her to myself for more than nine months.

Our house was crazy with activity when we came home from the hospital. A new baby, a new puppy, and a steady stream of visitors made for some exhausting days. But I knew that all of us were incredibly loved, including Wylie. He was so cute when we brought Melissa home. We put her in an antique wooden cradle in the corner of the living room, and Wylie would just walk up to the cradle to check her out or to find out what that crazy noise was when she cried. Sometimes he got his head caught in the rungs of the cradle because his beagle ears flapped back and wouldn't let him pull his head out. It was so cute.

Soon life was back to a new normal, and our baby went everywhere we did. One of those places was a new church that Dana and her husband invited us to come and visit, and we began attending Trinity Church of the Nazarene. The church had just broken ground on a new church facility. The gymnasium was the first building to be built, and that was where everyone started meeting. My husband, Dana's husband, and other friends who also went to the church helped build the new building on the new plot of land.

I loved everything about that time. I was experiencing things in church I had never known. There were impromptu prayers and praying out loud in front of the whole congregation. Many of these prayers were filled with emotion and even some tears. I knew already that I was an emotional person, but for it to be okay to express that emotion when you could pray prayers that were original and heartfelt literally blew my former Lutheran mind. The only place I had seen that kind of freedom in prayer was in the Sunday School class my mother taught at the Lutheran church. She even took prayer requests and prayed for them right then and there. I felt this same care and comfort at the Nazarene church, but there was something different.

At the Nazarene church, I felt a peace and almost a warmth. I felt comfort in those prayers that were so heartfelt and emotional. There was a family-like atmosphere that connected you personally to the people or situation you joined in prayer for. I began to feel a part of something like never before. I realized there was something I had been looking for that was fulfilled at that church. I felt part of a family, and I felt less and less alone the more I got plugged in. I began to stretch my wings, the kind that only God knew I had until that time in my life.

At the Nazarene church I began to learn just how special a personal relationship with Jesus Christ could be. I had always believed in God, and I knew the story and the words that were written about Jesus, but to start to really know Him and feel Him was spectacular. I met some of the most loving and godly people at Trinity Church of the Nazarene, and these people would become like family to me. I started singing in the choir. That was right up my alley. The chance to sing again felt wonderful. Dana and I also got really involved in women's ministry.

Shortly after that, I met a new couple—Darrel Tyler and his wife, Julie—who started coming to the church. They were long-time Nazarenes, and Julie and I immediately bonded and became very close friends. There was something about Julie that made me think of my sister. Maybe it was because she accepted me just like I was and would still sweetly try to guide me in ways that would soften some of my rough edges. Julie and Darrel were different from my ballfield friends. They were a little older, and I felt a real mentorship with Julie. She had hopes for me.

Darrel was a leader in the church and seemed to tame some of the rough edges of the men in the church. Julie had sparked a feeling in me to decorate my home and make a warm, peaceful place for me and my family. She also taught me a lot about entertaining friends in my home. I loved all this, and I loved having friends over. I guess you could say I began to recognize my spiritual gift of hospitality.

Chapter 4

Family, Firsts, and Fields of Dreams

L et's take a break from the story of my life at Trinity Church of the Nazarene. In the midst of becoming part of that church family, there was a shocking turn of events that happened in the family I was born into. I have mentioned the dynamics of being in my family with my dad as an alcoholic. Rarely could you know for sure what was coming next. My dad had gone through a hip replacement surgery and seemed a little changed in some ways. He really enjoyed being my Melissa's granddad, and she loved him too.

To recover from the hip surgery, my dad had to take a significant amount of time off from his job as the finance manager at a jewelry store. So, he was around the house more when we visited. There seemed to be less of the very hard, mean man he once was. He didn't feel very good in general after that surgery, and his health began to fail. Over the years, he had colon cancer. He also had serious heart issues that led to open-heart surgery. This time felt a bit different, and he seemed even more frail. Unfortunately, we got way too used to hospitals, and illness in my dad, but one thing took us completely off guard.

We had a tradition on Christmas Eve. Every year, no matter where all of us kids were, we came to Mom and Dad's house. We would get Mom and go to the Lutheran church for a late- night, candlelight Christmas Eve worship service. It started at 10:30 p.m., and we would welcome in Christmas at around midnight. But this year would prove to be different. The tradition would change in a major way.

My husband and I put Melissa in her baby's first Christmas pajamas and went to Mom's. That night would change everything I had known since I was a small child. I remember standing in Mom's kitchen, and Dad came in and asked a strange question. He said, "What do people wear up there at the church on Christmas Eve?" This may not seem strange to you, but I had never gone to church with my dad before, much less on Christmas Eve. Everybody who heard him say that were looking sideways at each other. Then Dad came down the hall to the kitchen and announced, "We'd better get going. We're gonna be late."

I thought Mom would faint, but she just grabbed her coat. We all followed her lead, silently got in our cars, went to the Lutheran church, and celebrated a very different Christmas.

After that strange Christmas Eve, my dad went to church all the time. We joined him and my mom back at the Lutheran church on Sundays. I really missed attending the Nazarene church, but we were still social with all our friends there. I missed my heart worship, but I was committed to making up for lost time going to church with my dad. I started to like my dad, and I could see myself loving him. Dad's hip never did heal completely, and in searching for a reason for that, doctors discovered that Dad had liver cancer. I was very sad about the possibilities for spending time going to church with dad being cut short. But on a lighter note, my family would be growing bigger soon. I was pregnant, and life continued to happen.

I was very overwhelmed at that time. I was dealing with the knowledge of Dad's cancer, raising a little girl who was barely one, trying to still work, and wanting to be there for both Dad and Mom. Dad continued to get worse. The time for conversations that were never had was now. One Sunday afternoon I was in the bedroom with Dad, and we were just randomly chatting. He talked about how he remembered what I went through when I had Melissa because he was there in the waiting room. That afternoon Dad asked me if I was scared that I would go through the same thing again, and I confessed that I was. Very quietly and sweetly, in a way I had never experienced with Dad, he put his hand on my growing belly and said, "I have had many surgeries in my life, but I have never had them put anything to love in my arms afterward, so don't be scared. You are strong. That is what I love most about you. You will be fine." In his own way, he tried to comfort me and relieve my fears.

Not long after that, Dad went down quickly. Mom did all she could to keep him at home. We all tried to help Mom with his care. One Sunday afternoon, I was at their house trying to help Mom treat a wicked bed sore on dad's backside. I was seeing my dad in so many ways I had never seen him before, but the worst was that he was completely helpless.

All those years that I didn't even like him—and loved him only because I knew it was the right thing to do—melted away in mercy for Dad and a feeling of sorrow for Mom that this was now her journey in life. I believe I forgave Dad along the years for his hateful behavior toward us because I could blame everything on his disease of alcoholism. But at this moment, he was not a monster. For the last year he had tried to mend fences with me by sharing the heart I had yearned to see when I was a kid. Was his encouragement about my C-section what I needed to grow into a strong, confident woman? No, not exactly.

I was so glad that I had that special moment with my dad, unfortunately, it was a little too late to help me, and what I had learned from him was to hide from my truth and build high, protective walls so high that few could climb over them. These walls looked very beautiful because they were covered in roses, but they were mingled with huge thorns and poison ivy. If you were among the few to get close to me, it was probably because you had walls just like mine and believed your walls would protect and hide you too.

When Dad died, I was five months pregnant for the second time. Melissa was 18 months old. The day we buried him was a cold winter day. I think I mourned all the things I had missed out on by not having the dad I wanted or needed in my childhood. I was now the person that missing these things had made me to be. So, I pulled myself up, took my toddler, and went home.

The next few months, I tried to stay close to Mom, but it seemed like she was going to be fine. It was apparent that Mom had managed everything about their home and her life, and she was used to it. Soon, she started growing some friendships beyond just on Sundays. She started going to a seniors' group at church. They had luncheons, fellowships, and field trips. Three months after burying Dad, it was on a field trip to tour a nuclear power plant that Mom had her first chest pains. A couple of heart catheterizations, a couple of stints, and a couple of open-heart surgeries would follow. But Mom was tough, and by this time she had retired from two jobs. After a time in cardiac rehab, she got one more job at the cardiac clinic and stayed there until she retired for the third time at 77 years old. During this time, Mom also battled breast cancer and melanoma. I may not have had as much intimate nurturing from Mom, but I did learn how to be strong, tough, and to trust the Lord from my Mama.

Psalm 34:18–20 says, "The LORD is close to the brokenhearted and saves those who are crushed in spirit. The righteous person may have many troubles, but the LORD delivers him from them all; he protects all his bones, not one of them will be broken." I would bet money that Mom called on this scripture many times when she had no idea how she would go on.

My second daughter was born in May right in the middle of what Mom was going through. Mom was there to welcome Megan into this world. Even though my blood pressure parked me in bed again for a month before she came, Megan's birth was much different, and I picked my delivery date. In definite contrast to what I went through the first time. I showed up to the hospital at 10:30 in the morning, and with Carolina Beach music playing in the operating room and me telling jokes, Megan was born at 12:53 p.m. Psalm 127:3–5 says, "Children are a heritage from the LORD, offspring a reward from him. Like arrows in the hands of a warrior are children born in one's youth. Blessed is the man whose quiver is full of them. They will not be put to shame when they contend with their opponents in court."

When Megan was about 6 months old, I became self-employed as an owner of my own cleaning service on November 1, 1988. That offered me many conveniences. I was able to be a part-time, stay-at-home mom. It was possible for my sweet girls to not have to be in daycare full time, and I had the flexibility to do things for others too. But I panicked if I lost business, and we struggled financially. I got so tired of being in and out of those seasons of fear that I decided to commit my business to the Lord. I said, "Lord, if you still want me to be in this business, give me what I need."

God answered this prayer repeatedly. Sometimes before I even had time to pray the prayer, He already had the provision waiting for me. It was often during those times of lost business over the years that God had arranged for me to be there with my mom or a sick child, or to chaperone a field trip. And time and time again I would be in awe when new business came on the same day I lost some. My business flourished. Philippians 4:6 says, "Do not be anxious about anything, but in every situation, by prayer and petition, with thanksgiving, present your requests to God."

Doing things for my mother branched out to doing things for my mother-in-law. Every Friday the girls and I would take Maw Maw (southern for Grandma) to the grocery store. Every week, the girls would hide in the back of my little station wagon and jump out to surprise Maw Maw. They loved that, and she did too. She adored them both and loved any kind of time she got to spend time with them, to hear them laugh or buy them a treat at the grocery store.

Maw Maw lived in a kind of rural area of Charlotte. I will never forget going there to pick her up one sunny day. She was watching the girls since I had to work. Later, I was told a story about Maw Maw chasing "the biggest rooster ever" away from Megan and the additional tattle from Melissa that Megan was hard-headed and wouldn't stay away from the rooster. Nonetheless, Maw Maw was able to save Megan from the rooster with her broom. We talked about that for weeks.

Maw Maw was born and raised in an even more rural place, and she had to quit school early to help raise her siblings. That made her tough and one of the best cooks I had ever had the pleasure of sitting at the table with for a meal. Maw Maw was as stubborn as she was tough, and she loved her own cooking. But then she got diabetes. One morning when I repeatedly couldn't get her on the phone, I drove to her house, but I couldn't get in. I investigated through the front window and saw her sleeping on the couch. But she wasn't moving when I banged on the window. I quickly called 911, and we discovered that Maw Maw's blood sugar was over 800.

Maw Maw was rushed to the hospital. She would go there again and again after it was discovered that she had severely damaged her kidneys and bladder. Repeated incidents like this one took a toll on her, and infection in her bladder sent her to the hospital one last time. She became septic from the infection, and it took her life. She died only a few days before her birthday, as well as Melissa's. They had the same birthdays. We did follow through with Melissa's eighth birthday party. I took this really hard because Maw Maw was a constant on my Fridays. It broke my children's hearts to be without her. But I know Maw Maw may be looking down on us now while singing gospel songs to the Lord, just like she used to sing to my girls. I was so blessed to be a blessing to this strong, sweet woman who once complimented me by saying, "She sure did keep her kids clean." Thanks, Maw Maw. I miss you.

Melissa and Megan both started playing softball at the local Optimist ballfields. It quickly became evident that Megan would excel at the sport and almost any that she tried, and she was so stinkin' cute in her tiny uniform. My girls are as different as night and day. On a softball field, Melissa was in the outfield fixing her ponytail, but Megan was behind the plate as catcher, practicing spitting through her catcher's mask. She knew the game and the tactics at a very young age. I remember someone commented on how cute Megan was behind the plate singing the song from the children's show *Barney and Friends*. I told her what they said about her being so sweet, and she said at the ripe old age of six, "Aw, Mom, it's not cute. It's distracting the batter." By the way, Megan went on to play in college.

Megan and Melissa both also played soccer and swam on our neighborhood swim team. Melissa exceled at swimming the way Megan did at softball. That girl could swim like a fish and was super competitive. She took all those swim meets we went to very seriously. She was also very versatile and quite the actress. She would star in many of the church productions and go on to be in her performing arts school productions.

As Mom got more and more independent and seemed to be embracing her new normal, my family decided to go back to the Nazarene church some Sundays. It felt like an unspoken need in my heart was being filled whenever we were there. I believe this need may have been something I was born with, so when I wasn't experiencing what was very organic in me, I was a bit lost. I was learning what a merciful, loving God we have, and my crazy life thus far had only started to shine a light on how much He loved me. From there on, the light would shine on me just as brightly as His mercies for me.

Chapter 5

Failures, Gifts, and Holy Kinship

Thank you for hanging in with me through the amount of personal history in the last four chapters and what my life looked like. I believe our lives can have some significant building blocks that God can use to build our testimony. It's just like the Old Testament of the Bible is a historical retelling of God creating the whole world. The lives of Adam and Eve and their story tell the ancestral history of God working in lives. Those lives later came together to be the building blocks of the time in history when Jesus came to be born of the Virgin Mary and began His earthly human history. For this I am literally eternally grateful.

I am always amazed when God can be seen in my history, in both subtle and profound ways. I have spoken of being drawn to a deeper, more participatory, more personal relationship with the Lord. I made up my own term for this—heart worship—to describe the closeness I discovered when I started learning how to do my own personal prayer. That was when I allowed my emotions to be part of a deep friendship with God, Jesus, and the Holy Spirit. Through this new closeness, I began to see a change in me that I had not yet recognized as the building of my own testimony. At times, that pull toward my relationship with God was the only thing I felt completely sure of.

Life together for me and my husband kept us on our toes. I was growing my business in a dramatic way. The kids continued to play sports. We were into softball, soccer, and swimming. We were financially stable enough to spoil the kids. At times we were at some sort of sports facility six days a week. And did I mention that my husband began to coach the girls in softball and continue to play himself? We were back and forth from the Lutheran church to the Nazarene church, but I just didn't have the heart to tell Mom that we were thinking about leaving the Lutheran church. So, we stayed Lutherans and were active there. At one point or another, my husband and I served on the church council. I sang in the choir and taught the youth. We looked like the perfect family.

We were so busy that we were both on autopilot in everything we did, including our marriage. We swept so much under the carpet because we just didn't have time to deal with it. Looking back, I can see my business being a way to avoid the problems between us. We hid a lot from most people, but not my mom. You may remember that she had gained a freedom to make friends after my dad passed. She had friends who loved her, and because of her, they loved us. We were at a breaking point in our marriage when one of Mom's dear friends at church gave Geofrey and me a weekend away. We accepted the tickets to a marriage retreat and apprehensively went away for the weekend. We let all those balls we had in the air fall to the ground.

With every breakout session we attended, we were instructed to go back to our room and discuss it. Some of them seemed pointless to us, and we didn't really take them seriously, but there was one that was very deep and emotional. It unearthed things we didn't even expect to come to light. If I remember correctly, it was about how our relationship with Christ influences our marriage.

I felt the drawing of God that day. I think we had an argument, but the most vivid thing I remember was locking myself in the bathroom and just sobbing uncontrollably. As we began yelling at each other through the locked door, I screamed that I felt like God could never love me since I had that abortion when I was 17.

God was so real at that very moment. I was on my knees on the bathroom floor, and my husband was still on the other side of the door. He said, "Who do you think you are that you could do anything that would overpower Christ's sacrifice on the cross?"

I don't know how this affected him at the time, but I continued to sob and ask the Lord to forgive me and come and be the Lord of my life. Right there and then, heart worship became permanent, and I felt free. I can't recall anything after that except that I believed the whole purpose for that weekend happened for me on that bathroom floor. I realized that the previous condition of my life was what bound me to my sin. But it was my belief that change was on the other side of my surrender that made me desire to acknowledge my sins and repent of them. That surrender opened me up to receive the Lord's gift of my salvation. I heard a definition that said that salvation comes with the knowledge that the cross is your unlimited gift card, but you must cash it in. There's a decision you can make that you will never second-guess or regret, and that's the one to follow Christ. It will surely end well.

I had worn that scarlet scar on my heart for so long, as well as all the other sins I needed forgiveness for. They were all part of my own personal condemnation. My mistake was that I filtered everything—especially who I was—through it, and it held me captive. That day, my whole identity changed, and I became a new creation. I saw everything differently.

Ephesians 1:5 says, "He predestined us for adoption to sonship through Jesus Christ, in accordance with his pleasure and his will." The plan God designed to happen that day was my adoption. I finally belonged. I mean I truly belonged to someone—God. As I write this, I see that scripture in a whole new light because I had never felt like my existence made anyone happy until then.

I was so busy after that weekend. My cleaning business was extremely successful, but when I lost accounts, I went into a panic. Gain and loss are a constant in my type of business, and those highs and lows are exhausting. I had not yet learned to trust God with my everything, so I didn't have the tools to head off the panic.

One day in utter frustration, I began to pray. And I reminded myself that I told God, "Okay, Lord, if you want me to be in this business, give me what I need." I must tell you, from that point forward, God continued to provide for me through that business. In my down times, it still never failed that my down time would be the time my mom had a health issue, or the girls were sick or had a field trip that needed a chaperone. God continued to show Himself faithful for me and provided for me personally. When I lost an account, there would be a call on the same day that would turn into a new account. There were even times that I had a job on a waiting list because I was so busy, and they were wanting the very time on my schedule that had just opened up. It is true that God goes before us.

During this time, we were still attending the Lutheran church, but the Holy Spirit began to speak into my life. The first time I experienced this I was driving some distance to a job. I had the radio on, and it was tuned to a country music station. But I heard what seemed to be an audible voice say these words: *Isaiah 43*. I looked down at my radio, and it was still tuned to the country station. I quickly turned it off. But I heard it again. *Isaiah 43*. Okay now, this was weird. I decided that when I got to my job, I would look up Isaiah 43 in my client's Bible. At that point in my life, I had no idea what Isaiah 43 said or even where Isaiah 43 was in the Bible. Most if not all my experience with the Bible was with someone else doing the reading. When I got to my stop, I found out that Isaiah 43:1-3 started like this:

> *"But now, this is what the LORD says—he who created you, Jacob, he who formed you, Israel: Do not fear, for I have redeemed you; I have summoned you by name; you are mine. When you pass through the waters, I will be with you; and when you pass through the rivers, they will not sweep over you. When you walk through the fire,*

you will not be burned; the flames will not set you ablaze. For I am the LORD *your God, the Holy One of Israel, your Savior."*

That was the very first time I had heard the Lord speak literally or audibly. I was thrilled and overwhelmed at the same time. I felt a pull to start reading the Bible for myself.

I went to the Lutheran church a bit longer, and soon after this event, the church got a new pastor. He was younger and a bit different, and what had happened to me didn't sound like the craziest thing he had ever heard. The first week he was on the job was when Hurricane Hugo came through Charleston, South Carolina, and continued up our way, plowing through the Charlotte area. It didn't break up until it hit the mountains in western North Carolina. It was a Category 1 hurricane even by the time it reached Charlotte with sustained winds of 90 miles per hour.

My husband thought I was crazy when I told him before we had any idea that the hurricane would affect us, that we should prepare for the hurricane with candles and extra water and food that didn't need to be cooked. Looking back, that might have been my first incidence of having any kind of discernment. Hugo would be the cause of a tornado coming through my neighborhood and right through our front yard, completely cutting off four trees at the same exact height. We were without power for weeks.

We cooked many things on a gas grill in the backyard and invited people over for meals. People also came to our house to take showers because we had a gas water heater. The new pastor and his family came to our house for dinner. They were welcomed by our three-year-old Beagle, Wylie, who humped the pastor's leg. The welcome to our home could not have been more embarrassing. Pastor Gil was a good sport, but we never lived that down. Pastor Gil brought a fresh spirit to the Lutheran church I grew up in. Church became a lot less by the book. He also introduced my husband and me to a movement in the western district of North Carolina called Via de Cristo, which means the Way of Christ. It was a spiritual retreat weekend that fed my hungry spirit.

After the retreat weekend, those of us who attended met weekly in prayer fellowships called Fourth Day meetings. Symbolic of the next day after the weekend was the fourth day of our new spiritual commitment. At those meetings, we not only prayed but encouraged each other in the lifestyle and fellowship with like-minded people. It was not an exclusive retreat. As a matter of fact, we were encouraged to tell others about how the weekend made us feel closer to Christ and each other in a way that made us want to come back and serve in our church.

My heart felt alive, and for the first time I felt some nurturing of my salvation. As my husband and I started to support the weekend community, we were eventually asked to be part of the teams that worked on the weekend and made the whole experience happen for other people. I started to feel closer than ever before to where I thought God was calling me. The weekends were separate for males and females, so I got to minister to women. That felt very natural to me for a direction I might be made for in women's ministry. I was on a quest to discover what was missing in my life, which seemed to answer that search for the time being. I wanted to find what God's will was for my life, and I was truly and totally exhilarated that it felt like He had a call for my life. I was reassured by what I read in 1 Corinthians 2:9-10, "What no eye has seen, and what no ear has heard, and what no human mind has conceived the things God has prepared for those who love him. these things God has revealed to us by his Spirit. The Spirit searches all things, even the deep things of God."

As there were more and more opportunities to serve on Via de Cristo teams, my faith grew more and more too. I relived the experience I had in my car with the declaration of Isaiah 43. And with every prayer time in a Via de Christo weekend, we made a request like this: "Come, Holy Spirit, fill the hearts of your faithful, and kindle in us the fire of your love." I could feel that the Holy Spirit was stirring again in my heart, and He certainly revealed Himself in my car that day and on those weekends through watching lives be changed.

I can't say I had become an expert at recognizing a move of the Spirit, but I know I heard an audible voice in my spirit and possibly my ears in my car that day. I learned that voice was leading me to the encouraging words of the Lord. They were words that told me that God would be with me no matter what. That day the Holy Spirit connected with my hurting spirit, and I felt so close to the Lord, Jesus, and the Holy Spirit, and I wanted to share that with other women on every subsequent weekend that I worked with Via de Cristo women's retreats.

I was astonished one day when I was walking from my car to my house and heard what was becoming a familiar voice. I clearly heard these words: "You will speak to many people in many places about me." I nearly fainted dead away, but I knew from recent utterings that these words were from God for my encouragement and for His glory. First Corinthians 2:13 says, "This is what we speak, not in words taught us by human wisdom but in words taught by the Spirit, explaining spiritual realities with Spirit-taught words."

It wasn't long after that day that I received a call from the woman who was the director of the upcoming women's retreat weekend. She was calling not only to ask me to be on the team for the next weekend but to be one of the featured speakers who presented one of the talks for the sessions. I was so excited to be trusted with such an important job for the Lord. On past weekends, I had spent hours talking to the ladies on a personal level, teaching, serving, encouraging, wiping tears, and holding hands. All I could think at that moment was, "God, is this where my call is to begin? Thank you for trusting me to draw others like me to You."

It was hard to believe that He chose this broken life to represent Him. I would later understand how personal this call would become. I would also learn how much Satan wants to put stumbling blocks in the way of our leaning into God's plan for our lives.

Chapter 6
Coworkers, Conviction, Damsels, and Destruction

I immersed myself in the work it takes to be on a Via de Cristo team in a different capacity. There is a lot of preparation when you are chosen to speak on one of these weekends. You must be committed to staying within the parameters of the subject matter of your talk. Another responsibility is to be a strong voice at the table you are seated at with five other women. It is your job to motivate and lead the direction of the conversation, all the time trying to stay undercover as an ordinary participant on the weekend. You are revealed as a leader when it is your turn to speak. By being vulnerable, a successful leader at a table helps the other women trust and allow themselves to be vulnerable too. That creates an atmosphere of safe sharing in hopes that the women at your table will feel free to share their hurts, scars, and traumas that may be healed by God's presence on the weekend.

After weeks of study and spiritual and mental preparation, I was ready. I knew the workings of my job inside and out. Just like Moses, I understood who I was in this kingdom-building endeavor. It was all because of God's grace that I had the strength and confidence to do what I was called to do on this retreat. We as a team knew what 1 Thessalonians 1:4–5 meant. "For we know brothers and sisters loved by God, that he has chosen you, because our gospel came to you not simply with words but also with power, with the Holy Spirit and deep conviction."

This was a big commitment for a mother of two little girls, seven and nine years old. It took a lot of sacrifice for my family every time I worked a weekend that went from Thursday to Sunday. This was especially challenging because my husband had gotten a new job as a butcher for a local grocery store chain a few months earlier, and his hours were all over the place. He also was working a part-time job for FedEx unloading airplanes at the airport. My business was a feast-or-famine kind of thing, and there were also all the sports we enjoyed. I was stretched thin. Like Lazarus' sisters Mary and Martha (Luke 10:38–42), while I was on a weekend or preparing for a weekend, I was more like Mary consumed with sitting at the feet of Jesus.

I did very little of the housework and meal preparing that Martha begrudgingly did. When the weekends with their mountaintop highs were over, real life pulled me back to a place I viewed as much less holy and far away from Jesus. But how important does God believe the family is? I was on a collision course of some sort, but I wasn't prepared for what happened next.

When you are two unfulfilled, stressed people like my husband and I were, you can begin to see that person you chose to do life with as the source of your stress and unhappiness. Most people try to do whatever it takes to fix whatever is wrong, but I didn't see what was right in front of me. Unhappiness and stress can get deep inside you if you let it or look to a person to fix it for you, and that goes both ways. And what you filter it through is crucial. This wasn't my immediate response. My ultimate response was to completely blame the offender.

Blame is an easy tactic, so you don't have to take responsibility for your actions. Stress short-circuits things like compassion, appreciation, and kindness very quickly, and I am no exception. My mouth can be the vessel God uses to glorify Him, but it has quite regularly been used to vent stress, fatigue, disappointment, and ultimately fear, and shred the person closest to me. You may have a clue as to what happened, but don't get me wrong. I am not excusing choices my husband made, but I was not completely without responsibility. I was a less-than-desirable mom and wife. But I was all in for my chance to present the Lord to those women on the retreat weekend. James 3:1–2 says, "Not many of you should become teachers, my fellow believers, because you know that we who teach will be judged more strictly. We all stumble in many ways. Anyone who is never at fault in what they say is perfect, able to keep their whole body in check."

James meant my mouth too. James 3:7–10 says this in the Message Bible: "This is scary: You can tame a tiger, but you can't tame a tongue—it's never been done. The tongue runs wild, a wanton killer. With our tongues we bless God our Father; with the same tongues we curse the very men and women he made in his image. Cursings and blessings out of the same mouth!"

I don't want anyone to misunderstand what I am about to tell you. The rest of this story is in no way meant to be represented as God's handiwork. It is quite the opposite. It was the work of the devil, but he was given the perfect inroad to get between me and my husband. Stress, fatigue, and filling our lives with busyness was the perfect way to make our marriage vulnerable to a turning away. It also proved to be the perfect way to sabotage the direction I was called to go in to have a glorifying life devoted and surrendered to God. Instead, my private behavior was anything but glorifying to God, and so was my husband's.

While my husband was working during the day and at night with a woman who had nothing to do with his stress from our home, he saw her as greener grass. But it was only the mud and muck of sin. I'm not entirely sure how long this was going on. With only two weeks until the next women's retreat where I had a coveted position to present a talk that might change a woman's life, I unearthed his infidelity quite by chance. I was devastated. The godliest woman I knew I could count on was the leader of the upcoming retreat, and I called her and asked if I could come to her house to talk. This was not unusual because we were friends by now from all the time we had spent preparing for the upcoming weekend. She certainly wasn't prepared for what I was about to tell her. She could not even expect this to be happening in my world because I was a totally different person in our personal interaction on the retreat team.

She was very compassionate to me in her counseling, but she asked me to give her some time to mull over what had happened. She loved on me for about an hour and then prayed for me to ask God what He wanted me to get from this devastating event. It sounded a little ridiculous to me that I could look for anything beyond my broken heart. I had not yet had a need to develop a habit of giving the devastating stuff to God. I was obviously also not in the habit of giving my stress, fatigue, disappointments, and fear to God. Now, I was completely broken and betrayed. Psalm 34:18 says, "The LORD is close to the brokenhearted and saves those who are crushed in spirit."

Those same days were filled with my husband's expressed regret, several arguments, and all kinds of bargaining for a return to normal. But one thing I failed to mention to my mentor was that I confronted the woman who was made of greener grass. I went to the store where she worked with my husband. She had no idea that I was waiting for her to leave work. For the next few minutes, I lost my ever-loving mind. There was violence and property damage right there in the parking lot. There was a threat that if she got up off the pavement where I had knocked her down, she would be sorry. I should have been arrested. I was definitely not the same woman who was preparing to lead other women to the Lord.

About a week after all this happened, I got a call from my mentor. She wanted to meet with me. I was so glad to have the retreat weekend to look forward to. I thought I was moving with ease from one compartment in my life to another. Not! The conversation we had again included hugs, tears, and prayers for me, but the bottom line was that the governing body of the retreat movement felt it best to ask me to step down from my position to present the message on piety. In Acts 10:2 and 7, the word *piety* is translated as "devout." This

Greek word means "to render to God the reverence and worship emanating from a holy life." Well, if I had read that, maybe I would have understood the far-reaching implications of me and piety.

The governing body of the retreat and my mentor were worried about the possibility that one of the women put in my charge for the weekend might have been a woman who was going through a similar betrayal, and that might totally derail the whole weekend for both of us and the rest of the table. I felt many things at that moment. I was angry at my husband for his bad behavior and for taking this from me. I was incredibly sad that because of something I didn't do, I would not be allowed to be used in God's service. And I felt so abandoned by my retreat sisters at the worst possible time in my life. I was completely defeated.

In Romans 8:28 Paul wrote, "And we know that in all things God works for the good of those who love him, who have been called according to His purpose." The "for my good" part I couldn't see. There were many things I had to work on, including the hypocritical way I was representing my life. Recently, my pastor, Michael Goins, said, "God's calling will stay on you, and even without repentance, it can't be shaken from your life." I did not yet know that, and I wish I did. But that day a tear fell and echoed through the halls of heaven.

Chapter 7

And Even the Saints Didn't See This Coming

After all the upheaval in our marriage, my husband and I decided to leave the Lutheran church and return to the Nazarene church with our friends. It seemed like the last bad decisions were easier to overcome when our saga of sin wasn't common knowledge with everyone we went to church with. I was still holding onto my desire to have heart worship back and have it in a place that would nurture heart worship in my life. I dove in headfirst to serve the Lord at the Nazarene church and be in the community that my spiritual soul deeply connected with.

We were immersed in our friend group, along with Dana and her husband. There were men's retreats and a men's softball team for my husband, and I was all about working in women's ministry. We, too, had retreats and outings together. We sponsored baby showers, wedding receptions, and anything social that went on at the church. It felt natural being back among these women.

The retreats we went on were usually at the Myrtle Beach area of South Carolina. We had stayed in more plush settings, but I think we had the most fun when we stayed in a retreat center that had bunk beds inside and rocking chairs on the porch. The retreat fellowship was a great place for me to learn at the feet of more seasoned women of the church as they brought the devotions on the weekends. We also had a lot of silly fun. We sometimes laughed until our sides hurt and cried until we couldn't breathe.

As time passed, the younger girls moved into leadership roles. Women's ministry Bible studies were also a place where I learned so much more than I ever had in my life about God's Word and what it meant to have a personal relationship with Jesus. The Bible studies we studied were written and led by some of the greats of current women's evangelism such as Beth Moore and Priscilla Shirer.

We also studied *Experiencing God* by Henry T. Blackaby. It was taught by one of my very special mentors at the church, Teresa Williams. Teresa had some life experiences that she had come through with the grace and mercy of God. I truly admired her, and she made that Bible study come alive for me. I was so enthralled by it that I would take the book and my Bible to the neighborhood pool with me while I was hanging out with my kids. There is a principle taught in that study that says God doesn't really need you to help Him, but He does want you to ask or look for where He is working and come alongside Him in service of His plan. We just need to be available to partner with God in what He is already accomplishing on earth. Other than just being a terrific teacher, Teresa and her husband, George, were there for me and my girls during some tough times in life. They are still on the periphery of our lives now. George still calls all of us on our birthdays.

I thank God for the strength I gained in doing Bible studies together with Teresa and the women of the church. They most often became bonding experiences and part of an unspoken mission to reach out to the women in that church. For example, the standards for service that we learned in the *Experiencing God* study, helped us to come alongside each other to help, support, encourage, and love the women in our lives as we walked closer with God.

It wasn't just the women who were bonding and learning how to support each other and come alongside one another in faith. The men were doing that too. They started to be more than just softball teammates. You could see their spiritual lives growing dramatically. They also had mentors who were trying to lead them in the faith. They had Teresa's husband George, along with Bud Belk, and Odie Page—who were the seasoned saints. They did their best to gently nudge our men in the right direction. The men were also led in God's Word by Darrel Tyler, not only in Sunday school but also by the lakeshore with a fishing pole.

I also learned from Darrel Tyler's wife, Julie, that a devoted Christian wife makes their home a warm, peaceful, beautiful haven for her husband and family—and a place that could always host a group of friends with a meal at any given moment. Julie and I had a sweet supportive friendship that evolved with time and age. Julie had a discernment that was surprising. She saw things in my life that I should proceed with caution about.

There was a renewal of commitment among marriages and friends. My husband and I were in a very good place in our marriage. And even though we would occasionally go back to church with Mom at the Lutheran church, we were completely plugged in at the Nazarene church. Needless to say, I was in heaven. Our marriage was healing, and we even spent time in prayer together from time to time. We made altar visits together too. It seemed that my husband and I had overcome the detour that our marriage had taken. We were always very social and together with our church friends. We had developed friendships with godly people that we and our kids had a lot in common with. We supported each other in everything. We were strong for each other and strong in the Lord.

Ecclesiastes 4:12 says, "Though one may be over-powered, two can defend themselves. A cord of three strands is not quickly broken." There is strength in numbers, especially if one of your numbers is the Lord.

Tragedy, however, would come to the Nazarene church and test the faith of one of our families in a devastating way. The son of one of the men of the church was diagnosed with cancer around the 12th year of his young life. How this boy named James fought back against cancer was inspiring. His fight and his courageous story would prove to affect not only the Nazarene church but whole communities of people. James had been a baseball standout at the local Pop Warner fields. He was in after-school care at a Baptist church down the road from the Nazarene church. He had been part of a basketball league for kids called Upward Basketball at that same church. James was living a normal boy's life when cancer interrupted it.

The Baptist church joined us at the Nazarene church, in praying for James, his parents, and his older brother throughout his battle with cancer. But cancer would end up overpowering James, and God called him to a healing not meant for this earth. These two churches and all the folks that James' short life had touched came together for his funeral. It's hard enough to say goodbye to an adult or older saint, but it is agonizing to say goodbye to a life so young and vibrant. I do not know how his parents and his older brother got through it all except for the love and presence of God in their lives. None of us would have even imagined how this would affect the whole church the way it did.

Satan has no mercy on broken hearts. He notoriously uses brokenness as his playground. Jesus accurately references Satan as a thief in John 10:10: "The thief comes only to steal and kill and destroy." Satan is not omnipresent like the Lord, but he does have agents of destruction who troll the earth looking where there is a broken heart or a crack in our armor or relationships. I have always been that person who tried my hardest to fix whatever need I saw in those I encountered. I had not yet learned that not everything is my job or my business—only God's.

James' life and death brought many unexpected people together. After attending the funeral, a young single mom started coming to the Nazarene church. I greeted her as she came through the doors. I introduced myself and helped her take her two sons to children's church. I then introduced her to some of the other women in the church. We had become a real sisterhood there, and I felt like she might need a sister.

It was customary for the older couples of the church to invite the newcomers to their house or take them out for lunch after church. In the same tradition, my friend group grafted this single mom in and included her boys, who were the same ages as many of our children. It seemed very natural, and it satisfied my desire to try to fix whatever was wrong with her life, to invite her to hang out with the rest of the broken, crazy, loving families who were part of our social group. Her participation in everything we did became a normal thing, especially after we "kidnapped" her and took her with us to the women's retreat.

It was there that we thought we got to know her a little better. We were able to introduce her to many of the older generations and some of the other women who didn't necessarily hang out with us. She seemed to fit right in. After the retreat, we continued as usual to attend the men's softball games, have lunches after church, and hang out other times during the week as well.

When we went to restaurants together, we usually got a giant booth for the adults and a table close by for the kids. Conversations were varied at best, but they started to move away from conversations you would expect to happen at a table full of church friends. They were getting more and more racy. I can't say that my talk was always completely innocent. And then one night I couldn't believe what I heard in that large booth of men and women. I was completely uneasy when I heard our new friend boldly announce that she had not been with a man in over seven years. I was blown away, and the reaction I saw from all the men at the table is hard to describe. Some of the couples around the table had been married for 10 to 12 years. The marriages that had the normal ups and downs could be vulnerable to a statement like that. I could only imagine that there had to be at least one man who for a fleeting moment wondered how he could help with that problem. It is a sad fact that in very busy family dynamics, intimacy can take a back seat to day-to-day life. And in my marriage, we were still battling back from previous bad decisions. The looks on the guys' faces said volumes, and the woman automatically put their trouble radars up.

This woman continued to be part of our friend group. Her statement was mentioned once in a conversation among the other wives, but it was chalked up to her being just a little rough around the edges. But there was still the fact that all our conversations needed to be reeled in a bit. That would prove to be just the beginning of a scenario we had not predicted.

It soon became apparent that our new friend had an agenda. Even though all us women had invited her into our social group, she was beginning to try to move deeper and deeper into our families and home lives. One of the husbands who wasn't at all phased by her, nonchalantly announced that she had not only said the following statement to him, but he had discovered that she had said it to several husbands. It went like this: "If I could pick a father for my boys, it would be you." Wow! Was she ever putting out feelers. There were tons of red flags popping up, and they just kept coming.

One Sunday afternoon, she called and told me she would not be at church that night because she had to get someone to come over and put her mailbox back up after it had been vandalized and destroyed. My husband was completely sure that nobody could do that for her like he could. I don't know what I said, but he begrudgingly decided to let John Doe handle it for her. I'm not sure if this accident was bait or what, and I wonder how many of the other fellas got the same call. I kept trying to give her the benefit of the doubt, but my husband was suspiciously eager to be at her beck and call. She may have already figured out who was taking the bait because soon, all the calls to me were short and pacifying. She would bid me goodbye right before she asked to speak to my husband.

At this point, my spidey-senses were kicking in. In the weeks that followed, we moved into the Christmas season. I immersed myself in decorating, Christmas shopping, and the children's Christmas musical my girls and I were in. I was so busy that all those red flags could have been waving in my face, and I wouldn't have noticed. The woman decided to go back to her hometown, somewhere north of us, for Christmas. I will say it was nice not to have her around. But she called our home three days into her trip. She didn't even attempt to make conversation with me. She just skipped the "middle woman" and asked for my husband directly. When she was done talking to my husband, I got back on the phone and asked if she was all right. She answered that she was fine, but I had a weird feeling that I was intruding in some way.

The New Year that rolled in was 1999, and there wouldn't be much to celebrate. Ironically, the singer known as Prince had a song called "1999" that said to party like it's 1999. New Year's Eve turned out to be the beginning of a year that was anything but a party.

Chapter 8

1999—The Year of the Interloper

The definition of an interloper is one who thrusts themselves into a place without having the right. That pretty much describes what our single mom friend did when ordinary hospitality didn't satisfy her anymore. My friend, Julie Tyler, was the first to truly pick up on this woman's maneuvers that thrust her right in the middle of the men, even after being invited to hang out with the women. It became obvious that a woman's friendship was the last thing the woman was looking for. She came into our lives, and I was trying to help her fulfill what was missing in her life with my friendship, not my husband.

I am not a docile person by any means, and I took a stand after watching my husband chase after someone right in front of my face. Her opening had been the funeral of a 12-year- old boy. I feel certain that her original target was actually the heartbroken father. She missed the mark there and probably didn't want to wait for grief to destroy his marriage. So she must have seen a crack in my marriage from recent bad choices and then set her sights on enticing my husband.

While my husband was moving toward another bad decision, she stoked the flame by filling his head with what she had designed for her original intended target. She did not refrain from speaking very provocatively about her desires for our heartbroken friend. And when I discovered that my girls were right in the middle of those conversations, I was livid. It was the trigger that finally clued me in and pushed me over the edge. It became increasingly obvious that this woman knew no boundaries. I realized the little chippy had a plan to woo my husband and was filling his brain with lustful thoughts.

I finally had enough and told my husband we needed some time to ourselves to be alone as a family. I told him I thought it was in our best interest that this woman not come over to our house anymore. It took a couple days for my husband to respond to that, but his response was very fierce. He came at me with both barrels of indignant anger. After a heated argument during a call I got from him while I was at work, he told me I had an anger problem. Truthfully, I couldn't deny that, especially since I was fighting for my marriage and family for the second time. He told me I had exactly two months to get some counseling for my anger, or he was leaving.

I figured I could only benefit from talking to someone, so I went to counseling for six weeks. I can't remember if it helped me, but it could have just given him time to maintain his relationship with the woman. What I do remember was a Sunday that we went to church as a family, and on our way home, we needed to stop for gas. It happened to be about two months since he told me I had to get counseling, or he would leave. He decided that pump number three at the gas station was as good a place as any to announce to all of us in the family van that he was moving out in three days. We were all in shock, and I was blown away that he did that to my girls. In the next few months, it seemed like he had some kind of irrational authority controlling him. I thought I knew that down deep he had a great love for his girls that would bring him to his senses, but no. Now he just dragged them along with him on his weekends with the little chippy and her kids.

I had tried to be a good wife by making my husband look as good as possible in front of everyone, especially at church. I had no idea that would cause most people at church to think what had happened to us was my fault. The rumblings were that I had some kind of mental break with reality. It totally flabbergasted me that the church condoned the very public relationship between my husband and this woman. It hurt so badly that I quit going to the Nazarene church.

I was called on the carpet by the Sunday school superintendent for not bringing my girls to church on the weekends I had them. I had a good reason. The little chippy who broke up my marriage was teaching the teen girls' Sunday school class. Bringing my girls to that Sunday school class was never going to happen. That woman would never be allowed to teach my girls anything, not on my watch.

My sweet friend, Julie, gave me some advice considering the chatter that was happening at my expense. She cautioned me to keep my behavior above reproach so there could never be any truthful, accusatory finger pointed in my direction. First Peter 2:23 says, "When they hurled their insults at him, he did not retaliate; when he suffered, he made no threats. Instead, he entrusted himself to him who judges justly." God's Word and my friend Julie's advice were worth a try. Nothing would surprise me these days.

And without notice, it was over, at least for me. But the damage had already been done. The little chippy moved on to another marriage, and it was time for a new set of victims. Unfortunately, the next couple in her crosshairs was my best friend Dana and her husband. This had so many layers of horrible to it. She had just devastated my family, and now she was doing it right under Dana's nose. Bless Dana's heart, she continued to be nice to the woman and tried to keep peace. I did not get upset at this, even though Dana was one of my best friends, but that was how Dana was, and she tried to hold her tongue. I guess it was some kind of manly competition that prompted Dana's husband to jump on the same disastrous roller coaster as my husband had. It devastated his family and a friendship. My husband and Dana's husband were best friends, and their friendship just became collateral damage for the little chippy.

At this time, there were several other things that began to happen at the Nazarene church. It seemed that evil had an open door to many areas of ministry there. Satan has an incredible ability to ride on the backs of those who have no conscience as they work their schemes in God's house. The church is never exempt from these attacks. As a matter of fact, it is a prime target for Satan, especially if God's people are not as close as they might need to be in their walk with God. The discernment it takes to recognize vulnerability to an attack comes to those who are close to the Lord in the Word and prayer. They can hear the Lord speak, revealing truth.

Satan is a cunning liar. He can throw even the most seasoned saint off their ability to perceive evil when they are focused on helping someone who portrays themselves as a helpless single mom. The loving godly saints at the Nazarene church may not have seen such cunning deceit before this woman darkened the door of that church. I'm sure that trying to see the best in all people had clouded their human judgment. They just weren't expecting her to be as good at it as she was, and as it turns out, more than our Nazarene church had been her target zones— yes, zones. We discovered that she had been asked to leave several other churches in our area for preying on married men and their families. It was one of the most heartless, despicable things I had ever encountered. It introduced me to the lessons I would watch and learn about Satan and his demons and the overwhelming and confusing spirits that can deceive the hearts and minds of God's people.

I don't know how I found out about Dana's husband being the woman's next victim. It seemed like my husband had custody of most of our friends, so communication was often limited. You might say because of my perceived "fragile" mental state, I had been excommunicated. Talk about a church hurt. It seemed odd to me at the time, but I got a call from the Sunday school superintendent. She called to apologize about how she had scolded me for not bringing my girls to Sunday school. She even invited me to return to church.

At that time, I was looking for how to become stronger. Returning to the church would be hard but a great start. And what a sweet, in-your-face way to show up, put all the rumors to rest, and impeach the testimonies about my mental state. Yes, I'm human, so I got real pleasure out of this. But what I didn't get pleasure out of was what Dana was going through. Dana never left the church like I did, and the church members had no reason to question whether Dana had any fault in what was blatantly happening for all at the church to watch. She had a real strength and peace that I'm sure she had to dig deep for to remain in the middle of all of that. I was in awe of her.

My growing strength was a little green. I was just learning to live with it, and I can honestly say that strength was in the form of being able to withstand hard things. But when someone I love is hurt, that strength is not in the form of self-control. And remember, I was still learning about the fruits of the Holy Spirit. The first Sunday I went back to the Nazarene church was the first week for the new pastor who had taken over leadership of the church. Bless his heart (a Southern thing). My first Sunday back, I found out about Dana and her husband, and I was shocked. Now the whole apology from the Sunday school superintendent made sense. She didn't still think I was out of line to keep my kids away from the influence of the little chippy.

Dana and her husband were the church power couple. They were thought of as unsinkable until this horrible hurricane found a crack in their foundation and blew into their relationship. Dana was the church secretary, and her husband was a member of the board. But they were no match for the cunning, manipulative, deceitful, plotting spirit of Satan that now seemed to reside at the Nazarene church.

My second week back at church, I requested to chat with the new pastor and his wife after church. I have little or no problem cutting to the chase when it comes to trying to stop the damage being done to someone I love. I met with the pastor and his wife, who were very gracious to hear me out. I quickly voiced my opinion about what an abomination it would be not to do anything to stop the further progression of what had become an attack on the sanctity of marriage by this woman. The pastor assured me he would keep an eye on this situation but had to get his own evidence. I will never forget what he said next. He reminded me that it always takes two to tango. Oh boy, did I ever know that, and at that time I wished for selective stoning to be reinstated.

It was not an overnight solution. I continued to go to church, and for whatever reason, the woman and Dana's husband became the youth leaders. They took a group of kids, including my Melissa, to the beach. They returned to the church on the Sunday when there was an awards ceremony for the youth scouting program, and my daughter, Megan, received an award, but Melissa was nowhere to be found. I started looking for her and discovered she had been ordered by the little chippy to go out to the church van and clean it out. That was wrong on so many levels. Her sister was receiving an award, and she may have wanted to be there. Melissa had gotten sunburned on the trip to the beach, and now she was sweating buckets out there in the sweltering summer heat cleaning out that van. Need I tell you that I was beyond angry? I did manage to hold it together at that moment and brought Melissa back into the air-conditioned church. She protested all the way across the parking lot because she had been told she would get in trouble if she didn't clean the van.

The fire in me was a five-alarm when I heard her say that. We got through the ceremony and all the congratulatory accolades, and I got a good look at how badly Melissa was sunburned. I decided to take her to the ER to have her treated for the huge blisters that had formed on her little back, but not before I had a come-to-Jesus meeting with the little chippy outside the front of the church. I was blinded by rage, and I didn't care who heard me or who watched. It took lots of self-control not to tear her limb from limb right there at the church doors. Needless to say, my mouth spewed every thought I had harbored toward this woman while I had watched her manipulate my family and this whole church. This Jezebel spirit had been at work, and my family and my church were caught in the fallout. My frustration of not being able to do anything to stop it was expressed freely by the expletives that flowed from my mouth. People's jaws dropped all around me.

It seems to me that not long after, this woman was asked to leave the church. At the time I didn't know where she slithered off to, and I don't remember if Dana's husband left in the same direction. But Dana and I were now bound in a new sisterhood of women whose marriages had been destroyed by the same woman. Together, we supported each other and did the best we could to pick up the pieces of our two families. But there was an unfortunate residue that remained at the Nazarene church.

> *Scripture says in Matthew 12:43-45 (NIV): "When an impure spirit comes out of a person, it goes through arid places seeking rest and does not find it. Then it says," I will return to the house I left." When it arrives, it finds the house unoccupied, swept clean and put in order. Then it goes and takes with it seven other spirits more*

wicked than itself, and they go in and live there. And the final condition of that person is worse than the first. That is how it will be with this wicked generation."

The Nazarene church eradicated the sister of serial deceit, but it was not ready with a filling of God dedicated to never seeing that happen again. That was of no fault of the remnant who didn't realize how much possession was to come back sevenfold. It affected many parishioners who encountered the dominance of the primary spirit that had been brought into the church. It had entered horribly by using the death of a young boy. Satan looks for the brokenness in lives or churches to weave his way into a whole community. Revelation 12:9 says, "The great dragon was hurled down—that ancient serpent called the devil, or Satan, who leads the whole world astray. Then the dragon was enraged at the woman and went off to wage war against the rest of her offspring—those who keep God's commands and hold fast their testimony about Jesus" The interloper began as one form and then took on an entirely different, more profound form at the end.

Chapter 9

The Prowler That Remained

After all that evil, divorce, and betrayal touched that church, the Destroyer of lives and families was not done. The marriages that were not protected by a constant indwelling of God became prey at every turn. Youth pastors made less than stellar decisions. Another level of the pastorate was affected, and with that, another marriage in the Lord's service was not spared. As several of us moved on, word came of other splits among our friend group that had associated with the temptress.

It makes you wonder about the power of the evil spirits that motivated her. There was also a spirit of addiction that came upon that little Nazarene church and eventually claimed the lives of two young women with the devastating effects of drug abuse. That fractured whole families, from parents to grandparents, siblings to friends. Jealousy also took hold, and there were underhanded plots of elimination and conquest.

In my family, there was rebellion against rules and struggles to maintain order. Everything seemed out of order. Melissa battled me at every turn. She eventually chose to leave the home she grew up in and move in with her dad. It left a huge hole in our house and an emptiness that was at times really awkward.

I was broken and feeling very needy. I'm sure I put a lot of pressure on Megan by trying to make her my everything. The weekends she went to be with her sister and her dad seemed endless, and I was a total mess. I was back to my mission to find value and importance. I didn't know who I was anymore. I certainly didn't feel loved. I toyed with the idea of what it would be like to date again, but how or where would I start? And then something incredibly unforeseen happened. Remember Scott? High school boyfriend Scott? He had tracked me down. I mentioned earlier that he had a way of keeping up to date on what was going on in my life, and he showed up at my door. He informed me that some former classmates of ours knew how to find me and pointed him in the right direction.

At first, I was scared to even talk to him. He eased my fears by telling me he had always loved me. And he reminded me, he had named his first daughter after me.

Just that quick, I was enthralled at the prospect of seeing what could come of a grown-up relationship with him. It turns out that grown-up people have all kinds of ways to love you and leave you. In the same way they were as selfish kids, they are selfish adults. I fell hard into the feelings of being wanted again. But those feelings were not so enthralling to him. He had learned how to not commit, or to commit all over the place.

The next direction I took was also a surprise and happened at a neighborhood gas station. I hadn't forgotten how another event that changed my life also happened at a gas station. This gas station was the place I ran into another high school crush. Run. I should run. Run hard from high school love interests. But no. This one was worse, much worse. I tried so hard to fix him.

Remember Satan's minions that look for openings to invade? I held the door for them. He nicknamed me "the little church girl." That was very far from accurate. And how can you lead someone away from their unholy lifestyle when you are so unholy yourself? We had several talks about the time he had felt the Holy Spirit meet him at an altar when he was in rehab, the first time. That whole thing should have been a big red flag. He had learned to speak Christianese when he wanted to suck me in. I think he clung to me when he wanted to associate with a life that he thought reminded him of that encounter he had with the Lord when he was trying to change his life.

Because of my association with him and this lifestyle, I put my whole life and my relationships with my daughters at risk. I was far from being an example of a good parent, or a church girl. He was a very enterprising individual. That may have been because he had lost many jobs because of his addictions to drugs and alcohol. His most lucrative enterprise was selling a "natural" smoking material.

I hate to admit that I was in and out of his circles in one way or another for almost eight years. I would have my feelings crushed. I had money taken and not returned. I was cursed and even physically abused to the point of having battle wounds. I still bear the scars. Over and over I cried out to the Lord to deliver me from him and his world, but I was so broken that I had started to believe this was all I deserved and maybe my only chance at not being alone.

God is such a loving God. In those years, my God never left me or forsook me, but He did allow me to have consequences. The worst was the alienation of my girls. I still have residue from that to this day. I often left God and forsook Him. I treated Him like my personal rescue genie. But He treated me like a merciful, loving Father. For some reason, He was preserving this broken brat time and time again.

This time in my life, not surprisingly had a big example of His miracles of deliverance. Because of the "natural" business this person ran out of his house, there was a raid on the house on a night that I happened to be there. Everyone in the house except me was hauled off to jail. This rescue was a shock to me, but I count it among the many times that God may have saved my life. I often wondered, "Why, Lord, would I deserve for You to protect me like You do?"

Through my own deeds, I defiled myself. I brought shame, disgust, and potential harm to my children. Everyone I expected to heal my emptiness just oppressed me even more with the power I stupidly gave them. I have learned that condemnation labels you and attaches to you. Whether it comes from you or others who convince you to think less of yourself, it doesn't matter. If you let it, your past can cover you, and you will wear it all over you. It holds you captive. It gives others the freedom to treat you less than you deserve. But you will never conquer what you refuse to confront. And when it seems that there is nothing good in your life and all seems dark, that's a good indicator that you are absent from fellowship with the Lord.

I believe that the same spirit that warred against my marriage found a home with me. As I have said more than once, spirits that Satan uses to do his dirty work look for a broken person or relationship to inhabit this world, and I was prime real estate. I learned how to manipulate and try to control the addicts of one sort or another that I had been hanging out with. I, too, was addicted to my search for love. I continued to use men and be used by them. But there were times that I slowed my searching and retreated to my own home. It was my safe place that I had never allowed any other man to inhabit.

During one of those times, I met a nice man who was a manager of a video rental store. I was renting lots of movies and spending a lot of time wrapped up in a blanket hiding from my need to search. This nice man was so kind, and he wanted nothing from me except a laugh or two. When we started dating, he treated me like a lady. During this time, I think my kids even may have stopped hating me because they loved him. This man tried to care about me in a normal, wholesome way, but I guess that wasn't what I was used to. It felt unnatural to me, or maybe I really felt I wasn't worthy of this kind of relationship. Unfortunately, it never sparked for me. I had become used to feeling loved by someone who wanted to be physical, so maybe this just wasn't moving fast enough. Therefore, I didn't perceive a potential for a good relationship, or sadly I didn't know what one looked like. I was the one who ended the relationship with this nice man, and I probably hurt a good person.

I never had any problems getting attention for some reason. I'm not sure why that is because I'm not a Barbie doll or a beauty queen. I do, however, treat people with kindness and no judgment, and I can love big. I think I did things this way in hopes that I would be treated the same way. This was just the tip of the iceberg of the tactics I used to try to convince people, namely men, to pick me and keep me. But despite my best conniving efforts, I always seemed to have an expiration date for my usefulness in someone's life. My life in those years seemed to be lived in complete darkness. The people, the places, the actions during that time were not those of a respectable person and not an example of godly living. When I finally took a break from the constant hunt, I tried to get back into church. I realized it was the very place I needed to be to find some peace and rest.

The next relationship I had was with a man who was happy with me and my girls, and my girls were happy having him in our lives. With their approval, I went all in, but not with my heart. I was compromising my feelings so the girls would approve and so this man would approve of me. It appeared to me that this relationship was headed toward marriage, so I moved in with Al into a house he had built, and I had helped design. I was happy, and so were the girls. Better than that, they were happy with me, so we all moved into this brand-new house. It seemed as if I was finally on track to be headed toward a life I could be proud of. That Christmas, Al gave me a ring. But there was a consistent thing hanging over my head—the next shoe to drop, or in other words, my oh-so-familiar expiration date.

Out of the blue, even after I received a ring and Al and I had been together for almost three years, my dreams were shattered. Al announced to me that he had some land in the mountains of western North Carolina and had always planned to move up there and live in a camper while he built three houses and put them up for sale. I learned from him that he had lived in the house we built together long enough to sell it without paying capital gains taxes on the profits. So the roof over not only my head but also my kids' heads had an expiration date on it, too. Talk about being blindsided and feeling like a fool. I did indeed.

Al comforted me by saying he would help me and the girls find another place to live. He said this with zero regret, devoid of any kind of emotion. And to top it all off, he told me he thought it had been a good business deal for both of us. I bet there are very few women out there who can say when they have been dumped, and that they had been told they were a good business deal. It turns out it was good for Al because I had split the expenses of living in that house long enough to avoid capital gains taxes.

My mom, and probably many moms out there, said at one time or another, "Why buy the cow if you're gonna get the milk for free?" Thanks, Mom. Well, it was a good deal for him because this cow paid him for the milk. I hate more than anything to feel stupid, but I hate myself for being so stupid. I was embarrassed that this fiasco became my truth. The I'm-out-of-here conversation happened right after 2006 began.

Echoing in my head was a conversation with a young woman who was new to the Nazarene church. She said something to me right out in front of our house in October of the year before I was given my eviction notice. It really ruffled my feathers and made me feel so convicted that I had to talk to God about it. She spoke a prophetic word over me, that she believed God had a big plan for my life, but I would not get to live it out as long as I was living in sin without being married. I had thought that was a short-term situation, but I prayed about it anyway and told God that if I was not supposed to be in this relationship, then show me how to get out of it, and how I was to accomplish that. Well, I got answers to both prayers.

The next nine months were a blur, but I looked everywhere for answers to my housing problem. While this was going on, Al and I lived separately but under the same roof. He made an apartment in the garage and spent more and more time in the mountains of North Carolina planning his next money-making build. I looked and looked for a place to live. I trolled the real estate websites. I rode around in my car looking for possibilities.

Something took me on a drive into the next little town close to where we lived. I ran across a house that looked very much like what I thought I was dreaming of. I called and set up an appointment to take a tour. I loved it. But I soon found out that it was more house than I could afford. However, the people selling the house had another house in the same area that they would be willing to do a lease to purchase. Part of my rent would go toward the down payment when I got a mortgage to buy it outright. I planned to see it the next day. My youngest daughter would be at her college orientation, so I would go alone, but not before I recruited several friends to pray for wisdom for dummies like me.

The owners left me a code to the lock box to get a key to the house. I walked into this little cottage, and it was so peaceful. The light was streaming in the windows in a crisp fashion of an early fall mid-morning. It was an old house with a sweet little porch out front, right under the most beautiful 100-year-old maple tree. It was just beginning to get hints of red and orange. The backyard was huge and completely fenced in on all sides. It would be perfect for my two Beagle pups. It had three bedrooms, two full baths, a dining room, and an eat-in kitchen. And did I mention it had just been renovated and made beautiful? My visions of where I would put my furniture and what color I wanted to use in the kitchen were interrupted by Megan calling to say that she and her boyfriend, Andy, would be coming by to check it out with me when she finished orientation. It wasn't long before they got there. She was only a mile and a half down the road.

When they got there, I showed them around, and they seemed to approve. But Andy comes from a family of contractors, and he knows a thing or two. He began to look with experienced eyes and had very few negative comments. As he was looking around Andy noticed the attic stairs in the hallway. He pulled them down and went up to investigate. I held my breath and was hoping the prayers for wisdom would be effective shortly. Then Andy, in his peaceful, level-headed tone, said, "Take a look at what I just found up here." He brought down a very old, almost crumbling picture of Jesus standing at a door knocking. The prayer for dummies did work, and they were answered in a stunning way. It had been a while since God had spoken so loudly. But that day He answered the prayer I had been praying for almost a year when I asked Him to show me how to get out of the house I lived in with Al. Not only did He show me how, but He also showed me where.

We all may be yearning for something. I believe mine goes back to a lack of validation from my dad and seemingly feeling unimportant to my mom. I was looking for security and unconditional love. We often seek, beg for, substitute, or settle for less than what we ultimately need from a human. We need to remember that humans will always fail us and yield far less than what God says is possible through Him.

In the story in Acts 3, Peter and John encounter a man who was crippled since birth. His friends brought him to the temple gate to beg for money. He cried out to Peter and John for money. Peter said he didn't have gold or silver, but what he does have is the name of Jesus to heal him and bring him to his feet to walk. Peter told the onlookers that it was this man's faith that made him strong. It is Jesus's name and the faith that comes through Him that completely healed this man. That day I started to see what is possible when I look to Jesus to be with me, make me strong, and give me a new start, and believe I can pick myself up out of crippling circumstances and walk.

My daughters and I moved into this little answer to a prayer. The girls were independent of me by now so I had to be independent and do all I could to find my way alone for the first time in a while. But I needed to remember that I have a strong backer in my corner. All three of us were learning how to be grown-up girls.

Melissa had a job, was in dental trade school, and had a serious boyfriend. Megan was starting college, and shortly after, she and Andy would become seriously attached. I was still searching for who I was and had yet to understand who had the answer to that. I got plugged back into the

Nazarene church that had at one time started to change my life. My ex-husband was gone, and so was the destroyer of my marriage. I went back and found the same people I had left before, and they loved me through so much all over again.

We can't allow disappointment to become a stronghold. We need to take all our disappointments to the altar. We need to seek out a fresh encounter with our Maker and our Savior. Be ready for God to do a new thing. Isaiah 43:19 says, "See, I am doing a new thing! Now it springs up; do you not perceive it? I am making a way in the wilderness and streams in the wasteland."

I was ready for a new normal and less wasteland. I began to cry out to God and believe that He heard my cries, whether it was to know what He wanted me to do to turn my life back in His direction or how to push past my fears of the possibility that my being alone might be what He really wanted for me.

Chapter 10

Running Headlong into Insanity

I'm sure it was out of necessity that I threw myself fully into my work. Megan was busy in college with schoolwork and softball. My social life once again revolved around church and a ballfield. But there was still that nagging feeling of being incomplete without a partner in life. Nonetheless, I stayed busy and went on monthly outings with a group of women from the church. We affectionately called ourselves the Peeps. Dana was in this group, and so were several others I got to know through church retreats and Bible studies. Half of us were married, and half of us were single—divorced—but we all had children about the same ages.

I grew stronger relationships with those I had more in common with. I got to know Robyn, whose marriage had also ended in the midst of the Nazarene church. Dana, Robyn, and I became like sisters. We eventually started to break off from the women who were married and had much more in common with each other anyway. I truly believe it was an amicable separation. I treasure my sisterhood with Dana and Robyn to this day.

I was very busy following Megan around with her college ball team and sitting at the ballfield once or twice a week. I made some new friends, and we had softball and daughters in common. I met one mom, Kathy, who I had a lot in common with. Her daughter was Megan's best friend. We traveled together and shared our love-hate relationship drama about the coaches and common feelings about our ex-husbands and being divorced. We became really close, and after the girls graduated from college, Kathy decided to move to North Carolina from Georgia since her daughter had decided to start her grown-up life near the college. Her daughter had also found the love of her life.

Dana and Robyn also found their special forever men. We still shared the ups and downs of life every month, and our sisterhood lives on, but Kathy and I shared a camaraderie of a life choice to start checking out online dating. We then had some war stories of the dysfunction you can encounter while dating men you meet online. I give real kudos to those who manage to be successful at that. I think I can fairly say that for me and Kathy, it was not a stellar experience.

I still had that nag in my spirit to continue looking for the love I thought I yearned for. It started to emotionally and mentally affect my judgment and my morals. What was equally as bad was that I was living a double life of trying to convince myself and everyone else that I was a church-going, fully committed Christian. I will say that I "interviewed" a lot of online candidates, in many ways trying to find my forever man just like Dana and Robyn had. The online dating can become an obsession. It became that and more for me. It was a stronghold in my life. The more I "interviewed," the farther I drifted away from God. But I should have known that in God you can experience something much greater than lust can ever give you. Lust is temporary, but God is eternal.

> *Psalm 196:10-15, 39-43 says, "He saved them from the hand of their foe; from the hand of the enemy he redeemed them. The waters covered their adversaries; not one of them survived. Then they believed his promises and sang his praise. But they soon forgot what he had done and did not wait for his plan to unfold. In the desert they gave in to their craving; in the wilderness they*

*put God to the test. So he gave them what they
asked for but sent a wasting disease among them.
They defiled themselves by what they did; by their
deeds they prostituted themselves. Therefore, the
LORD was angry with his people and abhorred
his inheritance. He gave them into the hands of
the nations, and their foes ruled over them. Their
enemies oppressed them and subjected them to
their power. Many times he delivered them, but
they were bent on rebellion and they wasted away
in their sin."*

This was me. I would have a flash of spiritual conscience
and then come back to God, but I was looking for an on-
demand God. I had not yet learned to trust Him, much
less believe what I was worth to Him. But I was still facing
or not facing the demons in my life and continually being
dragged back into my way of looking for my worth. God
led the Israelites out of bondage, and they begrudgingly
went. They questioned Him at every turn, even though He
proved His love and power when they safely escaped the
Egyptians through the Red Sea on dry land.

They did not know or blindly trust His plans for
their deliverance. They wanted to write their own story.
Sounds just like me, huh? I knew of His power and
provisions. I knew His voice that called me to find a

Bible on my job and read Isaiah 43. His voice echoed through my spirit. I knew His voice that called me to my knees for my salvation, and I also knew His voice that gave me a glimpse of His plans for my life. So what was my excuse? I had seen Him provide for me and my girls during my divorce when there was a choice of keeping the lights on or having a full refrigerator. But over, and over, I chose to go my way without even consulting His plan for my life.

Was it because I was stubborn? Maybe. But I felt like I was a slave to the lifelong mindset that I didn't deserve more than what had always been my lesser portion. I didn't let go of my own control to recognize my inheritance as a child of the King.

I was stuck in a second-rate existence of my own making. This segment of my life felt like a never-ending journey of hurt and disappointment. I rode a hamster wheel of relationships that I thought could fill a God-shaped hole in my heart, which he placed there at the time of my salvation.

Salvation is not a destination; it is a journey. It is only when we open our eyes and our hearts to the love God has had for us since before we were born that we can recognize the emptiness and life-sucking substitutes we have been looking to for unconditional love. We try to take these people into our hearts, expecting them to heal an emptiness that only God can heal. People, all people, will fail you. But God is God, your Maker, and the Maker of the universe, and He will never fail you.

Jesus Christ is the only one who has ever worn skin and can save you for eternity. But Jesus didn't die so you would feel guilty. On the contrary, He died so you could be made whole. He died so you and I could be changed. 1 John 1:9 says, "If we confess our sins, he is faithful and just and will forgive us our sins and purify us from all unrighteousness." Even knowing this scripture from early in my childhood and even knowing right from wrong and good from evil, I had become a slave to the sin in my life. It was like Paul wrote in Romans 7:20, "Now if I do what I do not want to do, it is no longer I who do it, but it is sin living in me that does it."

I was desperate for the validation I didn't get from my childhood. That desperation led from one pit to the next. I've heard it said that the best way to have a hope of getting out of a hole that you dug for yourself is to stop digging. That is very good advice that fell on desperate, defeated, deaf ears. I told myself I would just use a smaller shovel. And with that, I slowed down the online dating. How would you feel if you had a friend or family member you had sown so much time and love into, and they would only come around when they needed something? For me and the Lord, I was that family member. I had treated God like a genie in a bottle, or I would come back when it was better than the deafening noise in my head.

I decided to calm down and get plugged back into the Nazarene church. I was going through the motions at the church, but I was committed to the ministries I was part of like women's ministries and the choir. Surprisingly, one night my daughter Megan and her now husband, Andy, said to me that their pastor at the church just down the road was starting a new sermon series on Wednesday nights, and would I like to come. I was part of so much at the Nazarene church and had friends and relationships there. I had no reason to think about going. but right out of the blue, without a second thought, I said yes.

If I remember correctly, the series with Pastor Tom at Harvest Church was about the Holy Spirit. The Lord called my heart to come away from memories that still had me captive in an open wound, at the Nazarene church, which was potentially a playground for Satan. I was only existing in my life with the busyness of all I had been doing to play church. I believe it was an empty attempt to heal. But just as a splinter in your hand or foot festers if it's left in your body, I was festering from so much dysfunction that had lingered in my heart at the Nazarene church. I didn't realize just what a dark place I was in until I went to the new, holy environment that Megan and Andy had invited me to.

I began to rest and ultimately heal. I had no job to do and no ministry to be plugged into to serve. I began to feel the peace of the Lord in my life and my spirit once again. I knew in my heart that Harvest Church would give me the dose of Pentecostal worship that God had prescribed for my soul. Although prayer was a strong aspect of the Nazarene church, I was saturated in it at Harvest. Never was anyone shy about coming around you at the altar to support you in prayer. There was a presence of the Holy Spirit that I had never felt so strongly before in my life. It wasn't at all anything disturbing. I was intrigued, and I felt invited to investigate it further.

There was a women's gathering I attended one Sunday afternoon at someone's house. There was a time of prayer that afternoon that felt so right. I had witnessed such times of prayer at church before. There were two, maybe three times that I watched prayers just like this at the altar. I thought maybe I just couldn't hear well, but I later found out that the words they were praying were those of someone who had been overcome with the Holy Spirit. They were praying in tongues over the person they were praying for.

They asked if anyone had prayer requests. There were a few specific requests, but they also asked if there were any unspoken or anonymous prayers, and I raised my hand. There was no hesitation of at least three women to pray over me. Only I knew that I was praying to be delivered from the darkness that I was walking in. Suddenly, I realized that Pastor Tom's sister, Michelle, was touching my back and praying for me in the tongues of the Holy Spirit. She didn't know me very well, much less what my prayer needs were, but at that very moment, I felt loved, and that God surely knew what I needed. Romans 8:26–27 says, "In the same way, the Spirit helps us in our weakness. We do not know what we ought to pray for, but the Spirit himself intercedes for us through wordless groans. And he who searches our hearts knows the mind of the Spirit, because the Spirit intercedes for God's people in accordance with the will of God."

I felt so seen and loved at that moment—because I was. I didn't know what or how to pray at that time, and neither did Michelle. But she made herself available to be a vessel for the Lord, and the Holy Spirit cried out through Michelle on my behalf. This time marked a change in my heart that I hadn't felt in a long time. I felt peace and love like I did at the time of my salvation. I was no longer consumed every day with my search for love. I slowed my pursuits for love drastically, and for an undetermined amount of time, I rested in my relationship with Jesus Christ. But letting go of my control has always been a challenge for me.

When we are controlled by a victim mentality, we would rather have the predictability of being stuck in abuse and disrespect because it's what we know and understand.

Sometimes when those old ways are so deeply ingrained in us, it's less scary than to receive the unfamiliar from God who offers us freedom through trust and surrender. My belief that I will only find true happiness in having a partner in my life is a total delusion. Why was it so hard for me to give in to the reality that a relationship with the Lord is the only thing that could fill that emptiness and desire for the unconditional love I had sacrificed so much for?

The feeling of being seen and heard by God was very strong, but I discounted it, believing that I must not have looked in the right place for the person of my destiny. He had to be out there somewhere. I am so sad writing this now to know how I completely missed the answer to what I had been looking for such a long time. So I opened up my dating app again and expanded my search territory.

Chapter 11

Mirror, Mirror on the Wall

Living in a state of exhaustion can motivate you to do one of two things: make decisions based on what you feel you know or make decisions out of desperation. But only with rest and restored peace can you get a clear head to make sound decisions. At that time, I had neither. Even though God was offering me both, I chose the path that was well-traveled. I thought it was the path of least resistance.

No sooner had I reopened my dating app with the extended territory that I got a message from the person in the first picture I clicked on. He was a year younger than I was and only about an hour away. He told me he was retired and a former Marine. My mind was racing. Was he retired from the Marines? Had he been so successful at something else that he was financially well off enough to retire early? Wow! This sounds interesting. And that Marine thing probably meant that integrity and toughness had been drilled into him, not to mention he was extremely handsome. The more we talked, the more I thought I had to meet this guy. It took only a few days before we planned to meet.

He came to me because for some reason, I thought it was too risky for me to go out of town to meet him. We planned it for a Friday, and early Friday evening turned into Friday at 7:00 p.m. He drove up my driveway while I was sitting on the porch. I walked out to his Dodge truck to greet him. He was very charming. He took my hand and in a very deep voice with a Southern gentleman accent said he was glad to finally meet me. He was tall, 6'3," and I like tall. Then he stooped down and kissed me on the cheek. That was different. We sat on my porch and talked until most restaurants around my house were closed, so we rode to Charlotte to one of the last drive-in restaurants around. We ordered our food from his truck and ate our late dinner from a tray on our laps. It felt very natural, maybe because this was one of my favorite places to eat. It was in my old neighborhood, and it has been part of my life since I was a small child. As we got to know each other more, we laughed and laughed, and we never ran out of things to talk about.

We got back to my little town just in time to close the local grocery store where we bought beer. We took the 12-pack back to my porch and drank, laughed, and talked till the rising sun changed the October sky from navy blue to orange and pink. Inside my house, we fell asleep in each other's arms. We continued the weekend on a repeat loop. And even though I told him I was a Christian, I knew I was sitting smack dab on the proverbial fence between heaven and hell. Revelation 3:15–16 says, "I know your deeds, that you are neither cold nor hot. I wish you were either one or the other! So, because you are lukewarm—neither hot nor cold—I am about to spit you out of my mouth."

Those who are cold have an opportunity to be influenced in a powerful way by the gospel. But those who are lukewarm or on that fence are in a worse condition than those who are cold. They know just enough about Jesus so they're not resistant, but they're also somewhat calloused to His voice. What God orders, God will pay for with his grace. But what God hasn't even been considered in, He is under no obligation to bless. God had planned none of this for me. No matter how much I tried to share my faith with Robert that night, I impeached my credibility as the sun came up the next morning.

Jeremiah 17:23 says, "Yes they did not listen or pay attention; they were stiff-necked and would not listen or respond to discipline." Stiff-necked means haughty or stubborn. It leads to disobedience. Exodus 32 says God saw what the people were doing. They had turned away from their Lord. The Israelites got tired of waiting to hear from God through Moses on the mountain, and they constructed their own idol, or god, in the form of a golden calf. They made plans to worship it since God wasn't giving them attention in their timing. I did the same thing. I went about my design for a relationship, motivated by desperation just like the Israelites, and it had nothing to do with God's design for my life. No matter how much I put Him and His Word in the sidecar of my life, I knew in my heart that was not where He should be.

For the next few days, I continued making bad decisions with Robert—in a blur of desperation. Within a three-week time frame, he had moved in with me. We drove to Georgia to pick up his stuff and so I could meet his mother and his two young sons who were five and six. We made that trip to Georgia monthly so the children could come back with us to stay for a few days or a weekend. Every month we dragged these two hurting little boys into our environment of confusion.

My girls were barely speaking to me, and I believe they surmised that I had finally lost my mind and proved myself unstable. I was starting to slowly realize that Robert and I were very much alike. We were two extremely flawed, broken people. Just like me, he used other things to forget his pain, and I used other people to distract me from mine. He regularly self-medicated with alcohol so he was not completely heartbroken from not being with his boys. I didn't help this situation at all because I had such a desire to finally have a partner to share my life with that I participated in his problems while trying to convince myself that it was all okay. I thought I might have found a person who would love me, value me, appreciate me, and stay.

This was a huge problem for us both because we were feeding off each other's dysfunctions. He was filling my unhealthy need by staying, and he was staying because I was signing off on his addictive behavior. When we looked at each other, we saw the same broken person looking back. It was like looking in a mirror, but you can count on your reflection in a mirror to move and cleave to you, and we could not reflect the other because we each were an illusion. You don't usually expect a stranger to have your best interests at heart, and the same became painfully obvious that we were motivated by selfish desires. Days became weeks, weeks became months, and eventually, even though we had been together for almost a year, we didn't know each other at all.

I learned shockingly just why he had "retired from working" when I witnessed his first bout with heart problems. It was so bad that it sent us to the ER. It reminded me so much of my childhood watching my dad suffer with his bad heart. It was only the beginning of living through cardiac scares with Robert. He ended up getting what would be the first of three stints in his heart, and with the addition of those three, they numbered in the double digits.

This happened soon after our first Christmas together. It was complete chaos because we had to depend on his ex-wife to get his boys here. That proved to be only the beginning of learning just how much control she would have over our relationship. The kids were with us until after the New Year, and during that time, my 94-year-old mom ended up in the emergency room very late on New Year's Eve. I got a call from my brother who lived with her that I might want to come. I got ready and headed to the hospital in the middle of the night. She had taken a fall that had caused a gash in her head.

The medical staff sutured her cut, got her stabilized, and made plans to discharge her. My brother told me he could handle getting her back home and I could go home, so I made my way back in the wee hours of January 1, 2015. Just as I pulled into my driveway, my phone rang. It was my brother. He said that when they were moving Mom from the bed to the wheelchair, she coded. She died right there in that same room where I left her semi-alert and talking. For what was only a few seconds I felt some joy for Mom, that her hard journey was finally over, and she was walking the streets of gold in the presence of her Savior. But my joy was short-lived when my brother said, "But they got her out of the wheelchair, and they revived her."

I know my mom had a DNR—do not resuscitate—in case of loss of life. I am sure my brother knew that, and I screamed, "Why did they bring her back?" He said he told them to. If I had not just gone through sorrow and a momentary joy that landed smack dab in the middle of shock, I would have been furious. I was devastated for her. It was not a joyful thing to me that Mom was yanked back from the glory of heaven.

Mom was admitted to the hospital, and for the next month she would be there in a cold, depressing hospital room. She had visitors, and sometimes she knew who they were and sometimes she did not. My brother, my sister, some nieces, and a nephew, and I stayed with her most of the days and into the evening. I took the evening shift because I had nobody at home at that time.

Robert thought he needed some space to sort some things out, so he took the boys back to Georgia, and stayed. This was not the first time he had taken some time away, but he usually only went back to his sister's house in Asheville. My days were such a blur that I don't even remember them. I was on autopilot, and I just did what I needed to do without much thought.

The evenings were challenging emotionally for me, and I sure could have used a shoulder to cry on when I came home each night. In the evenings, Mom's lucid times were inconsistent. There is something called "sundowners" that happens to the elderly when they are out of their normal element. They seem to be even more out of touch the closer it comes to bedtime. I saw this in the form of Mom being confused about where she was and who I was, which was very painful for me. But in contrast, she would have times in between when I would sing hymns and read the Bible to her. She would ask me some coherent questions like how each of us kids were doing. I would update her to the best of my ability. Then she would focus on me and ask how I was doing. I would tell her that I was fine and add some bits and pieces of my day. But Mom was not at all satisfied with my small talk about my day, and she would ask me repeatedly how I was doing, as if it was important to get at my truth about being alone. I know I had not mentioned that to her, but I think she knew I was sad, not only about her but because she somehow knew that something was wrong if Robert was not with me.

During this time, Megan's father-in-law, Jack, had a complication with a knee replacement. He got very sick from an infection in that knee after some dental work was done. He ended up in a sepsis state, had a stroke and passed away. This was an extremely sad time in my world, and I was on overload. I felt powerless to comfort Megan's mother-in-law or her family, but I tried the best I could.

Robert and I were still having phone conversations, and I told him that Jack had passed away. I asked if he would mind coming back to help me be there for Megan and Andy. But he didn't come back for a couple of weeks. He showed up the very day we found Mom a room in a senior facility near her home. I knew and others must have known that it would become her new home. Robert went with me that evening to see her. It was so strange but kind of made sense that Mom was overly glad to see Robert when he walked into the room. She held onto his hands and told him how relieved she was that he was back. That day was the first day in a long time that Mom had not asked me several times a day if I was doing okay. Maybe she finally felt at peace thinking I would be all right now that Robert was back.

We got a call from the facility at 8:30 the next morning that Mom had passed earlier that morning. I once again felt joy that Mom was free to be with her Jesus. But on the other hand, I didn't exactly have as much peace about Robert being back as Mom did.

On February 8, 2015, Mom woke up in heaven, not that senior facility. But we found out that she didn't make the journey alone. We discovered that my dear cousin Kathleen lost her husband, Will, to kidney failure, and he woke up in heaven that day too. As much as I wanted to be with Kathleen in her loss and she wanted to be with me through mine, we had to love each other through this from miles away.

There was a sweet funeral for Will at Jerusalem Lutheran Church in Rincon, Georgia, and one for Mom at Park Road Lutheran Church in Charlotte, North Carolina. It was such a blessing to hear the effect that Mom's life had on so many others. That day, I pulled through with the strength she had taught me. Two weeks later, Robert packed up completely and moved back to Georgia. I guess he figured that I couldn't continue to hold up his broken heart because I was holding up my own. Again, I felt completely alone.

The next few weeks, I begged, I argued, and I cried until I couldn't cry anymore. I resigned myself to the fact that I had to get used to my new normal. What I can see in hindsight is that if I hadn't still been looking through the eyes of desperation, I would have realized that my life was going on and I was depending on a strong person to get me through this season. That strong person was me.

Over the next two months, I started to enjoy my life. My new normal consisted of having Robert as my friend, not my love interest. I planned to go down and visit him for his birthday, which was five days before mine. I was running around getting ready to leave town and go south when I got a call from Robert. He told me to hold off on leaving home. I was suspicious and thinking anything and everything except the possibility of what I encountered when I got back home. I had hardly been home 15 minutes when Robert came rolling up the driveway with his truck packed to the ceiling and overflowing in the rear. It was filled with all he owned that he had taken with him when he decided to move back to Georgia. He walked over, sat down very naturally on the front porch, and announced that he had made up his mind that he was going to do everything it took to make our relationship work.

We fell right back into the same mess we were in before, but this time there was a new plan. I knew I was not happy in my soul about the way we were living, so with my desire not to be alone and Robert's plan to do whatever it took to make this work, we moved headfirst into a plan to get married on the one-year anniversary of the day we met. I thought at least then we would be living right in the eyes of the Lord.

Often, we think that a very dysfunctional situation is normal. We can begin to think it's God's will for our lives, especially when we are trying so desperately to redeem it in our hearts. I was so far out of living in the light that I couldn't see that I was living with something I shouldn't. I felt like I was broken and incomplete in the eyes of my girls and the world, even though I was about to be more "normal" when I had a brand-new husband. But worse than that, I knew I was broken in God's eyes. It didn't dawn on me that in God's eyes, I didn't have to stay that way.

I wished I felt that His thoughts were the only ones that mattered to me, but I didn't slow down long enough from doing everything I could, as fast as I could do it, to realize that my kind of broken was never going to be fixed by me or any other person or their opinions. In that same desperation, Robert and I married on October 10, 2015. I linked my life to a broken, unsaved man and forgot that even as broken as my life was that day, a perfect man died on a cross to redeem it long before I was even thought of.

That day was off to a stellar wedding day for me. The ceremony, as beautiful as it was, was shrouded in rain—literally and figuratively. We had a very nice reception after the wedding. Robert's family celebrated, my friends were happy because I had convinced them I was happy, my family was cordial, and that was the best I guess they could do. My friends Bill and Lourdes hosted the event at their home. They did a bang-up job allowing 40 people to gather in their home on a day that rained like there was a monsoon. My softball travel buddy Kathy made me a stunning wedding cake. My peeps Dana and Robyn have walked through so much with me, and this day was no exception because they stood beside me with a prayer in their hearts that this would turn out okay for me. As the festivities came to a close, I looked around for Robert and discovered that he had left me and his kids to go take his mom, his sister, and her son back to our house so they could head home. Man, I felt such déja vu. Forty-five minutes later, after a couple unanswered phone calls, I spoke to Robert and reminded him that he had left his kids and his new wife, and didn't tell us he was leaving. It seemed he had forgotten to come back to get us.

I could fill the next few pages with regrets, but getting left at the wedding was the beginning of a hopeless mess. I searched for the hope I thought I would feel after we married and began "living right" under God's marriage parameters. In Matthew 19:5–6, Jesus talked to the Pharisees about what godly marriage looks like: "For this reason, a man will leave his father and mother and be united to his wife, and the two will become one flesh. So they are no longer two, but one flesh. Therefore what God has joined together, let no one separate."

Very early on I began to question if God had created this marriage or if we had for the wrong reasons. I can't completely speak for Robert for why we married, but for me, it was deep down breaking my heart because of my disregard for all the Lord meant to me. Jesus also said that Moses permitted divorce because of the hardness of their hearts. It was just under the surface how hard both of our hearts really felt about this marriage. I hadn't found in our marriage the commitment I had always been looking for. And Because I didn't want to have to own another failure, I fought to maintain the source of my biggest misery.

A stronghold is something that holds you captive. Any kind of defeating captivity you put yourself through that does not build you up but tears you down can also destroy your peace. I think we are creatures who have an innate need for peace, and we can only survive without peace in our lives for just so long before the lack of it can start to agitate us with no solution to the problem. Again, I felt the calling to the Lord's sanctuary. The only times I felt happy and whole was when I was covered in God's peace.

Right after Robert and I got married, we started going to the Baptist church around the corner from our house. It was so close that we could see it from our backyard. I saw a glimmer of hope for us because Robert began to do his own search for God's peace. He took a real liking to the pastor of the church, and he loved the fun atmosphere that was a big part of the congregation. He too was still looking for somewhere to belong.

We made it to our first anniversary, holding on by a thread. We went through the motions of a celebration. But Robert was becoming more and more distant. He spent a lot of time on our front porch in hours of pondering. Little did I know that his looking for God was not driven by a desire to share a love for God together. He was in search for a way that God would console him in his homesickness. Ironically, that was the perfect place to be searching for his consolation, but he had not yet learned that.

We carried on with plans to go get his boys to come and spend the summer with us. But while he was spending time with his two favorite humans, his heart was more than figuratively breaking. He was having real pain from his very real heart issues. He ended up in the hospital for a heart catheterization of the artery called "the widow-maker." It's the main artery that pumps blood through the heart. He was very torn between home with me and home with his boys. The trips to take the boys back to Georgia to their home were getting harder and harder. All I wanted to do was be part of what could heal his broken heart. But I was not.

Life in our home was extremely tense. Robert began to resent me because he was so torn between trying to find some way he could fix me and give me what I was missing. And I was frustrated because I was doing all I could to try to make him happy and be enough for him. But I was fighting a futile battle. Robert had gotten a part-time job that filled the endless hours he was spending in his own head. It gave him purpose, and I was hoping it was making him happy enough to see a future with me. But his time away from work was spent with a beer in his hand and a longing in his heart. I'm not quite sure when it began, but while I was at work, he was spending some of his porch time researching ideas for how he could get back to his boys—who were the only thing that would fix and fill his heart.

I began to bargain with him that he could spend more time down with his boys if that would make him happy and more inclined to remain in our marriage. How sad that was. I was settling for much less than I deserved in a marriage, just to hold onto someone who was already halfway out. But that didn't fix a thing. Months later, I was exhausted from walking on eggshells, but I knew God could console me in my defeat. I was now bargaining with God to fix this. Little did I know that what was ripping my heart apart, God was going to use to call me back to where my heart could be free.

There was an upcoming women's retreat with the women from our Baptist church, and I was so excited about going. Robert offered me money so I could go on shopping adventures with all the ladies, but I didn't need money to sit by the ocean and be with the Lord and listen for His voice. I needed to find my center again. I had placed Robert as my center, and now I felt its futility. But even though I was afraid he would pack up and leave while I was away, I had an all- consuming desire to be with the One I knew truly loved me. And even though there was one last attempt to give me extra money, all I wanted to do was sit by the ocean immersed in prayer and get my own heart fixed and filled. And that was exactly what I did. The Lord met me by the sea and filled me with the Holy Spirit in such a way that He gave me the words to minister to the other women on what turned out to be a tumultuous retreat. I came back home with a new center in my life, and it would prove to be right on time. Imagine that!

Within a week, Robert announced that he had been making plans to move back to Georgia. I was broken by that announcement, and in the next two weeks I needlessly begged, reasoned, manipulated, and cried buckets to no avail. On November 10, 2017, I watched what I thought was my whole life drive away from my house. Ironically, November 10 was the date of my wedding day with my first husband. I should have seen this as an encouragement from God that I had survived before, and I would again. But God used an even more beautiful event to change the way I looked at that day forever.

A baby boy named Lincoln was born on the same day that Robert left. This precious baby would help heal my heart because I was asked to become his nanny. Intellectually, I remember the sadness of the loss of a love. But emotionally and spiritually, I began to be covered by the love that would prove to save my life. I never put that burden of being my new stronghold on Lincoln. But I felt such peace coming over me that I was able to recall the peace I felt as the waves crashed on the shoreline on that retreat a few weeks earlier. That peace was the love and healing of the Holy Spirit returning to be my center. It would become a love like no other that would once and for all heal my heart and fill the emptiness that had haunted me all my life. But I still had to realize that Robert was no longer anywhere near my center. I also had to learn that he was not even close to being my destiny. I was about to start on a path to self-discovery that would be my first stop on a journey to realize what was to become my real destiny.

Chapter 12

Messages, Meditations, and Margins

The Lord has never left me or forsaken me, not in all the painful times in my life that were caused by someone else or in the painful times because of my impulsive, bad judgment. To find some kind of direction, I was desperate to be in God's presence constantly. I depended on His every word. Again, I felt a confirmation that I was experiencing something natural. I now considered God and sought this input in so many ways. This new action proved to start a change in my life. The first thing I started to do was seek God in His Word. This may seem very elemental or even reckless, but when I did my devotions, I prayed first, spent time listening, and then held my Bible before the Lord, on its spine, and asked

Him to lead me where He wants me to read. I asked Him to give me direction or insight for my day, and then I just opened it.

Right after Robert left, I sat in God's presence one morning and just talked. Actually, I ranted. I may have believed that the anger would help me feel stronger. I told the Lord that Robert had been compiling a list of everything I had done to ruin our relationship. I was indignant that I couldn't have possibly had anything to do with the disintegration of our marriage, because I was the one who was all in. I sat still at the end of the rant, and as I did after prayer, I listened.

With help from the Holy Spirit, I believe I heard God say, "Well, let's talk about this." He continued to speak to my heart, giving me not so comfortable insight. He led me to Psalm 139:23–24. "Search me, O God, and know my heart; test me and know my anxious thoughts. See if there is any offensive way in me and lead me in the way everlasting."

I began to lay myself and my character totally bare before the Lord that day, and every morning after that, I asked for the same help, using Psalm 139:23–24. I don't know how long I did this. It was more than just days and maybe more than weeks. I sometimes also included that question in my journaling. It was painful to hear God's feelings about my character, but it was a healing and redirection that I can't imagine getting any other way. In the midst of this metamorphosis, I also asked God to speak in some other ways.

I wanted to give God the power in my life that was and is His by figuratively doing like Joshua did when he walked around the walls of Jericho. I took my marriage license and elevated it on a made-up pedestal on my dining room table. For six days, I marched around that table, asking the Lord to speak. On the seventh day, I marched around it seven times. Right after I finished that last circle around the table, I screamed as loudly as I could and then waited for God to speak. I believe He did because that was the day the electrician came back to fix the electrical issue on my front porch. Afterward, he told me about the end of his own relationship when God spoke to him and told him that he was worth more than anything the relationship had offered him because he was "fearfully and wonderfully made." By the way, that is from Psalm 139:14. I felt God answer my march around the table at that moment, but He was not done.

One of my favorite women evangelists is Priscilla Shirer. She is the daughter of renowned evangelist Tony Evans. After the visit with the electrician, I turned on YouTube and saw one of Priscilla's messages right there ready and waiting on me. It was the insight I needed to get my answer from the Lord about my marriage. Priscilla's message was called "The Sabbath Margin." I listened to the message and realized it was the culmination of the answers I sought while marching around the dining room table. It was the realization that the conversation I had with the electrician was a foreshadowing of what I would learn under Priscilla's teaching that night. I remember seeing God move for the benefit of my deliverance because I am worth more than Robert had ever seen in me. I needed what Priscilla described in her message. I needed to stop doing the same thing I always did, because it was not God's design for my life. I needed to recognize what God offers to me is more than anything I had been looking for in any prior relationship. He wanted me to just be and let him take care of the rest, just like he first commanded the Israelites.

We sometimes feel that when we have a chance to have some breathing room and yet aren't completely worn-out, that somehow, we have failed. This feeling of failure is just the way the enemy wants us to feel if we aren't spending every ounce of our energy trying to fix everything and everybody. Satan is against the rest that God wants to give us. We know the enemy loves to use our sins, failures, and faults to instill that feeling of failure in us.

But we must be on our guard by knowing what God thinks of us through a deep relationship with Him. We must recognize the schemes of the deceiver that try to make us doubt God can take care of all we need. We need to believe, and trust that He can, God led me to Luke 1:45, and I began to plant this in my spirit, and I wrote it in my journal like this, "Blessed is she who believed that what the Lord has said to her will be accomplished".

We cause a lot of our own problems by holding onto and devoting ourselves to things, people, and even our past for much longer than we should. It would be in our best interest to stop filling our lives with clutter. We become enslaved to this clutter instead of free in Christ. Jesus gave His life to save us from our sins, but He also wants us free from getting caught up in things that may become more important to us than He is.

God gives us protections to try to free us from distractions that separate us from His perfect design for our lives. We may have accepted these distractions for so long that we don't see the boundaries God puts in our lives for our guidance and protection. We need to trust our heavenly GPS so we don't waste so much time recalculating. We can become accustomed to the busyness in our lives that makes us feel validated, useful, or important. Busyness can be an idol if we don't hear God telling us to stop and trust. We can't imagine not doing what we can to hold onto control. Any idol is a real problem. Exodus 20:3 says, "You shall have no other gods before me." But if this idol is motivated by a desperate need for love and acceptance, it could leave us duty-bound to whatever or whoever the validation may come from.

I had become duty-bound to Robert in that empty, toxic marriage that should have never happened. It wasn't until later that the light bulb moment glared in my face, and I recalled the words of Jesus about His plan for marriage in Matthew 19:6. "What God has joined together, let no one separate." But the truth was that God had not put our marriage together. We were just scheming with each other to get what we thought would heal us. I was stuck in a giant hole full of dysfunction, digging deeper and deeper in search of love and acceptance. Then God showed me that the way to get out of the hole was first to stop digging and then to look up and see that He was waiting on me with a rope. He always had been, and He had a plan to show me the freedom I didn't realize was already mine.

Just like the Israelites, I had become used to being a slave. It has been said that God took the Israelites out of Egypt, but He had to work to get Egypt out of them. I had been doing the same thing over and over, expecting different results. This phrase has often been deemed to be the definition of insanity. God wants us to walk through our lives in freedom. Galatians 5:1 says, "It is for freedom that Christ has set us free. Stand firm, then, and do not let yourselves be burdened again by a yoke of slavery." You can stand firm with confidence by trusting the Lord and surrendering to His design.

God has told us to stop our laboring and trust His plan and provisions. God created the original design for this when He instructed the Israelites through Moses. In Deuteronomy 5, God creates instructions through boundaries for us. It's called the Sabbath. In Deuteronomy 5:12–14, God told Moses to tell the Israelites, "Observe the Sabbath day by keeping it holy, as the LORD your God has commanded you. Six days you shall labor and do all your work, but the seventh day is a sabbath to the LORD your God. On it you shall not do any work." The definition of sabbath is a day of rest and worship on the day of the week that commemorates the day God rested after creating the world. The Sabbath provides balance. The definition of balance is to keep or put something in a steady position, so it does not fall.

On that day, I tuned in to hear Priscilla Shirer deliver her message, "The Sabbath Margin." It was the culmination of how God was working in my mess and answering when I asked Him what I should do about my crumbling marriage. But He also used the affirmation I heard through the electrician who shared his story of realizing that he was "fearfully and wonderfully made" and worth more than what his shattered relationship had given him.

God wants us to have margins in our lives where we can stop toiling. God wanted me to recognize that He wanted me to rest—from people-pleasing, from wondering if I am enough, from the worry of saying or doing the wrong thing that would set someone off, from the fear and panic that I felt when I thought about when my next expiration date would occur. I needed to know what it meant in Exodus 14:14: "The LORD will fight for you; you need only to be still." I needed to stop what I was doing in my marriage and recognize that enough is enough. All I had been doing ended with having nothing to show for how hard I had been working to get, have, and save my marriage. I started to take hold of the fact that if I just rested, recuperated, and looked up, I would see that the love I had searched for all my life was right there on the other side of my trust, and it was all I would ever need.

I would never try to tell you that everything from this point on was rainbows and unicorns. But in the down times that continued to find me, I was no longer feeling alone. I had learned how to rest in my sabbath margins and trust that God would provide when I stopped trying to gather or fix it. I was learning how to surrender. What most people don't understand about the place you surrender is that it is a place of beautiful, peaceful, restful freedom. I began to exhibit this more, but there was another big situation ahead where I would need to draw on my trust in the Lord.

On the Saturday I had to shut down my crafting business venue, I acted much like the world would toward my landlord. My daughter Megan witnessed this, and she aired her disappointment of me. But worse than that, she gave in to her desire to let me know how much I had disappointed her with my bad outbursts of anger and also as her mother because I had sought after one man after another to satisfy what I had been searching for. She told me there had been many times in these pursuits that she had been scared for my safety. She had worried about me in ways that someone's child should not have to. I was indignant about this at the time, and it led to nothing good. We had a what we call in the south, a knock-down drag-out fight.

I was hurt, but I didn't realize that these deep feelings inside Megan had been hurting her for so long. God had a huge job ahead of Him to bring me to a place where I saw His love for me and surrendered to Him completely, and let him govern my responses in all situations— whether dealing with people in the margins of my life or hearing the brokenness in the hearts of both of my girls when they gave me a chance to be accountable to what I was responsible for.

The night after my war of words with Megan, I felt like I was broken beyond recovery. I texted my pastor at the Baptist church and told him I felt like I had no hope. He listened to what had happened, but he didn't pipe right up and give me some sage advice. He reminded me of who God was in my life and the fact that I was way too blessed to be spouting such nonsense. He told me to look at the blessing of what Megan said—that she loved me so much that she feared the way I was living my life. He said to take that as motivation to call her, beg for her forgiveness, and share with her what God had been doing on the journey He had recently been taking me on. I tried to call Megan, but she would not answer. I knew what my assignment was, and I would never give up on completing it so Megan and I could begin to heal.

I woke up with a new light in my heart. I went to church and sang the praise and worship songs with new commitment. Then Pastor Jason started his series on the Holy Spirit. These kinds of messages always interested me. During his message, I felt the Holy Spirit moving in that church. In the prayer after his message, the Spirit came over me, and I began praying in tongues. But when I realized what I had done, I put my hand over my mouth and squelched the Spirit.

As church was letting out, a visiting couple a few rows behind me came up to me. She said she had seen what had happened to me in prayer and encouraged me to lean into that. No one else remembered seeing that couple in church that Sunday, and like Mary in Luke 2:41–52, I pondered this occurrence in my heart. Mary's thoughtful reaction to the events around her showed their importance. Something else shifted for me that day. As if on cue, Pastor Jason came running into the sanctuary as I was chatting with friends. He yelled, "Sally, come quick." My response was, "Okay. In a minute." He countered with "No. Now. Come quick." I hurried out the door. Pastor Jason pointed up to the sky and said, "Look." Right above the church was one word from someone who was skywriting. The word was HOPE.

Nobody ever found out who did that. I even asked the pastor if he had done this, and he said, "I didn't do this. Get real." I have a picture of the word HOPE in the blue sky over the church. People also saw it in five other locations that day. One of those was over the funeral of a young father who had died from cancer. So I ask you, Is God real? Yes! Does He hear us when we cry out to Him? Absolutely! Can He make His presence known to us in ordinary and miraculous ways? Without a doubt! And I have the picture to prove it!

Chapter 13

It's All About Perspective

The Apostle Paul wrote in his letter to the Corinthians about the Lord's all-encompassing love for us in times of trouble. Second Corinthians 12:9 says, "My grace is sufficient for you, for my power is made perfect in weakness." Paul continued to share a reminder of God's presence and favor on us in our weakness, sadness, and pain—mentally, physically, or emotionally. Paul went on to write in verse 9, "Therefore I will boast all the more gladly about my weaknesses, so that Christ's power may rest on me." Verse 10 says, "That is why, for Christ's sake, I delight in weaknesses, in insults, in hardships, in persecutions, in difficulties. For when I am weak, then I am strong."

This turned out to be the best advice and encouragement ever for me. At this point, I was weak, but I was learning how to be strong in the knowledge of God's power dwelling in me. This would begin a refresher course in knowing and growing into my true identity.

There have been many occasions where I have seen God work in mighty ways, but I have also witnessed His miracles in my life. I have had a cleaning service since Megan was six months old, and I have clients I have worked for more than 20 years. I also worked for a couple for over 30 years. I believe I spoke earlier about how blessed I was in my business. One large blessing is that I became part of the lives of my customers in a way that made me feel almost like family.

Vance and Delina Furr were one of those families. When I met Vance and Delina, she was teaching high school history, and Vance worked in state law enforcement. She is a tiny little person who married a very tall, bigger-than-life kind of man. I would guess that she would fit under his arm. They shared a love that many will never find. But cancer is not a respecter of persons, even a very large one, and it is not a respecter of love either. Vance became ill, and many doctors investigated what was ailing him. But it was an oncologist who would become Vance's main doctor.

The love between Vance and Delina was legendary to those who knew them. It was certainly one I longed to find. Vance's health would be scary for a while, and then it would rally. We would all have hope, but that hope would be short-lived. As Vance's health declined, I spent a lot of time at his home, and one day he came into the house without my knowledge, and I was singing a praise and worship song to the top of my lungs. I was surprised and embarrassed until I realized that this was the beginning of a sweet relationship based on our mutual love of the Lord and the music that celebrates Him. Vance began to spend more time at home with me while I cleaned. He was becoming weaker and weaker.

I came into their house one day carrying a heavy burden of serious prayer for my eight- year-old niece who had just had a liver transplant, and her recovery was having a big setback. Vance was right there to encourage me. I told him I had called my sister, her grandmother, at the hospital and told her to post Jeremiah 29:11–13 over Hayleigh's bed and speak it over her. It says, "'For I know the plans I have for you,' declares the LORD, 'plans to prosper you and not to harm you, plans to give you a hope and a future. Then, you will call on me and come and pray to me, and I will listen to you. You will seek me and find me when you seek me with all your heart." Vance agreed that was a great scripture to pray over Hayleigh, and she came through this set back very quickly.

Vance also told me that he thought that was an excellent idea for himself, and he was going to give it some thought.

He tipped his baseball hat at me and went down the hall. As he left, I thought he could probably teach me more about the Lord in our short times together than I had learned in all my 50 years. I also figured that Vance had prayed a lot of scripture over his life in the past, and he was very familiar with the habit. But this dear man and great mentor encouraged me that day and made me feel that I had originated that plan.

A short time later, Vance called to tell me he had found his scripture. It was Isaiah 53:5 (NKJV), which says, "By His stripes we are healed." I told him that was the best one ever. I wanted that to be the source of Vance's earthly healing, but I suspected it was the encouragement Vance needed to remind himself of the source of his ultimate healing.

As Vance continued to decline, I happened to be at their house on Delina's birthday. Vance asked me for a favor. He said he couldn't believe he had forgotten Delina's birthday and could I go get her a card. He wanted it soon so he would have it by the time Delina got home. I made a quick phone call to my daughter, Megan, who was closer to town and could get a card quickly. She bought what Vance called a beautiful card, just what Delina deserved. That pure love touched me and Megan deeply that day.

Vance held onto his hope as long as he could. But cancer continued to ravage his body, but not his spirit.

He was failing quickly. Delina and I discussed their regular cleaning over the next few days. She said I should go ahead and come because she was sure it would only be a few days before family and friends descended on their home in bereavement, and she wanted to be ready. When I arrived, Delina confirmed that hospice had advised her that Vance was not long for this world. She added that he had not been awake in days, and it would be fine for me to clean their bedroom because he would not know I was there. I tiptoed into the room as quietly as I could and without bursting into tears. I was trying to be very quiet, and then I heard a voice. "Sally, is that you?" I took a deep breath and said, "Yes, Vance, it's me." and he responded, "By His stripes, Sally, I will be healed." I said, "Yes you will, Vance. Yes, you will." Those were the last words Vance spoke before he went home for his healing.

The first part of Isaiah 53:5 (NKJV) says, "But He *was* wounded for our transgressions, *he was* bruised for our iniquities; the chastisement for our peace *was* upon Him. And by His stripes we are healed." I believe this was the part of the scripture Vance clung to completely, that Christ paid it all so he could get his ultimate healing and spend eternity in God's presence.

I had been blessed to be mentored by Vance Furr. I was equally blessed to see God put people in my life and my business to fellowship with. I had such beautiful opportunities to watch Him work, hear Him speak to me, and confirm me in my job and how He planned to use me through it.

I have learned many different things from all my customers over the years. I have seen births and deaths. I have worked for the women of three generations of a family. I have worked for dedicated Christians and been mentored and encouraged in my faith along the way. I still work for Vance's wife, Delina. We share some very deep discussions on how best to live in this cruel world and hopefully represent Christ. But I have also worked for people who are not Christians or those who may have strayed from their Christian walk.

Deborah and her husband Larry were also my customers. I can see how God had a plan for me to be in their lives. I met Deb when her granddaughter and my daughter played travel softball together when they were preteens. I hadn't been in business very long when I first started getting to know Deb at the ballgames. I am a talker, and one day at the ballfield, I told her I had a cleaning service. It was not long before I was working for Deb and Larry in their home. I quickly learned that Deb was a boss at work and in life. She had been through some stuff, just like me. She intimidated me at first. But after getting to know her, I realized we were very much alike. She had her street credentials, and I had a good bit of them too. She quickly grafted me into her life and became one of my greatest cheerleaders. I began allowing her to mentor me in being a strong woman and embracing who God had made me to be. This training came at just the right time. Imagine that! And the direction of our friendship would go on an even more important journey.

Life is always ebbing and flowing, and when Deb's employer changed, she decided to walk away from her job. I was put on hiatus with cleaning. But that would prove to be short-term. When I lost a major account in my business, I scrambled to make ends meet. I called all my old clients and networked through friends and family. So I called Deb and asked her if she could put me back to work. She announced that she had been thinking of calling me for weeks. It turned out that Deb needed me because she was battling the aftermath of breast cancer. I went back to work for her weekly. I was asked to do regular cleaning every other week and special projects on the other weeks. This routine lasted several weeks. As I was always accustomed to doing, I shared what was going on in my life and what God was doing in the midst of it.

Those project weeks began to be filled with Deb wanting me to just sit down with her to talk and drink coffee. I felt a bit guilty at first, and then God showed up in this plan. Deb asked me if I would be willing to bring my Bible to read with her. That evolved into studying God's Word together and having deeper conversations about the Lord. Deb shared with me that she had been saved when she was younger, and she had a deep yearning to revisit that chapter in her life through our study and conversations. A few more weeks went by, and I got the news that my heart was scared to hear.

One morning, we sat down with God's Word, and Deb told me she needed me to pray because her cancer was back. It was now in her liver. I knew the path that liver cancer can take, especially since the liver filters the blood. It was liver cancer that took my dad in a matter of weeks. God was with Deb and me in meaningful ways until she began to fail quickly. I had a suspicion that she was a lot sicker than she disclosed for a longer time than she had told anyone. The last day I spent with Deb was when Larry had to go on a road trip to deliver one of their precious French Bulldogs to someone who had time to help this dog have her puppies. On that day, whenever Deb was awake, I read the Bible to her. She would try to talk to me, but she spoke in a way I could not understand.

Deb passed away a few days later. She made sure she passed into the loving arms of Jesus while we talked about our Lord. When I came to visit her family at her home when they were receiving friends, I shared the story of how my special project days became sharing the Word with

Deb over coffee and how she had shared her salvation story with me. Their eyes became misty, and their faces were full of shock because none of them had a clue that this was Deb's back story and now it could become a legacy for all who heard it.

I continued to work for her husband, Larry. He was a very hard sort of man with a heart that had been melted by his love for Deb in a way I had never seen. He told me that Deb had made one request of him during those last few months. Her request was that he stop using the Lord's name in vain. He told me he was trying but that he was not religious.

Over the next eight to 10 years, Larry talked about his desire to see Deb again. That opened the occasional door to conversations about where Larry thought Deb was now. His answer was always that he knew she was in heaven. I began to talk to about where he stood with his faith. He always told me he wasn't religious like me. I told him I was not religious either, but I have a personal relationship with Jesus Christ. He would say, well you go to church all the time, and I am too bad to go to church. I replied that he could have a personal relationship with Jesus, too, and it didn't only happen if he went to church like me. I told him if he asked Jesus to be part of his life, then Jesus would do the cleaning up for him. The many short, gentle discussions evolved into conversations that would lead me to ask Larry who he thought Jesus was. When I told Larry the story about the day I saw the word *hope* written in the sky, I told him nobody ever found out who did that. Larry raised his voice and emphatically said to me, "Now Sally, you know who did that. It was God!"

Larry started to exhibit signs of aging that looked like the onset of dementia. But that didn't happen before he got to tell me that it was God who made all things like heaven, earth, animals, and man. He said Jesus was God's Son and that He came to earth to die on a cross for our sins and rose from the dead three days later, and that Deb was in heaven with Jesus. I think Larry believes what he needs to in order to be in heaven with Deb and Jesus. At least I pray that he does.

The Lord has used me on several occasions to bring His story to others. I didn't know anyone could hear me when I was singing in a restroom I was cleaning for work. My friend Julie who worked in the office across the hall heard me. It reminded her of her church roots, and it persuaded her to return to church after being away for some time. She rediscovered what she had been missing in her life and committed her life to Christ. She invited her live-in boyfriend to come to church with her, and God met him there at an altar. After that day, they wanted to honor God, and they got married. They began taking her grandchildren to church with them, and those children and their parents received the gift of their salvation too. None of this was about me. It was because God used the fact that the restroom had fantastic acoustics, and I was praising Him while I worked to be the chance Julie needed to hear God call to her.

I have continued to be the person God made me to be, just like Deb encouraged me to be. I have never been perfect, as you have already read, but I know the One who makes me perfect in my weakness. In 2 Corinthians 12:9–10, the Apostle Paul wrote, "But he said to me, 'My grace is sufficient for you, for my power is made perfect in weakness.' Therefore I will boast all the more gladly about my weaknesses, so that Christ's power may rest on me. That is why, for Christ's sake, I delight in weaknesses, in insults, in hardships, in persecutions, in difficulties. For when I am weak, then I am strong." I ask the Lord every day to show me my purpose for that day in His kingdom.

I remember a tale of a young girl who had the most spectacular head of hair. This young girl was hospitalized because she was sick and going through chemotherapy for cancer. She had the most positive spirit. Despite her illness, she tried hard every day to remain positive. Every day she styled her beautiful hair. Day by day, she would style her hair even though she had less and less to work with. When the full bouncy curls were no longer possible, she switched to putting her hair in bouncy pigtails. The next day, she could no longer do pigtails, so she pulled her hair into a ponytail in the middle of the back of her head. She did this as long as she could, but eventually she had to comb her hair over the top of her head into a side swooped ponytail. The next day she could no longer cover her head, so she added a bow to what was left hanging at the back of her neck. Not surprisingly, the next couple of days seemed so sad to all around her when she didn't have any hair left to even use a bow. But she got up the same way she always did with that positive spirit of hers and said, "Oh well. At least I don't have to style my hair today." I try to remember this tale of the girl with the beautiful hair who knew that it's all about perspective.

Chapter 14

Finding My Purpose and Walking in My ECHO

When God calls you, He calls you according to your gifts and potential, not your past. But with the understanding of Romans 8:28— "And we know that in all things God works for the good of those who love him, who have been called according to his purpose"—we can also know that He can use our past in any way He has prepared. I want to thank God with all my heart that because of Jesus's saving grace, my life still has purpose even after all I have done. I believe in Romans 5:8 that says, "While we were still sinners, Christ died for us." And, While I was still a sinner, and destined to sin again, Christ died for me. He deserves the title "the Most High" in my life because no amount of judgment from any person, no amount of guilt from myself or others, no amount of fear in my life, and no amount of misguided plans that I made have deterred God from having a redeeming, incredibly beautiful plan for my life. He confirmed this in a whisper into my spirit that simply said, "no matter what." He made real to me the comforter, the perfect guide, who is mine in the Holy Spirit. It is the Holy Spirit who has had to remind me many times of who I am and whose I am.

One of the reminders came slowly and subtly into my life. As I said before, I immersed myself in study under many godly women evangelists, both through Bible studies and listening to podcasts of their messages they had presented all over the country and the world. One of my earliest was Beth Moore. I had studied under her many years ago, and in the midst of one of her presentations on television, she challenged her listeners to start praying for a name that meant something between only them and God. It was a reference to the story of Jacob wrestling all night with what he thought was an angel, but it was God. At the end of their confrontation, God told Jacob that He was changing his name to Israel. I imagined that would be a cool thing to have God answer a prayer from me to change my name to something else that only made sense to God and me. I prayed this prayer for what seemed like months, and truthfully, I had almost given up.

One day I took my car into a local dealership to have my oil changed. They put my car up on a lift to do the job, but they stopped short of the oil change and came to speak to me in the waiting room. They informed me that I had bigger problems than just my oil. They told me that one of my front tires was so dangerous that they could not in good conscience allow me to drive the car away from the dealership without fixing it. I didn't quite believe them when they said that because I had made a 20-minute trip up a busy interstate twice a day for three days to do a dog-sitting job. So they took me to my car and let me see the tires for myself. There were actually two tires that were bad. I told them I had another tire at home for that car and could just run home a couple miles away, pick it up, and come right back. They said they would have one of their service associates drive me home.

In the 10 minutes it took us to go to my house, I had a conversation with this young man who was driving. He shared that he was going through a heartbreaking divorce that would take away a young boy he had been a father to almost since his birth. This young man was almost in tears. I did the first thing I knew to do, and that was to ask him if he knew the Lord. He said yes, and I told him my divorce story and shared that if it hadn't been for praying to God to bring me through that time in my life, I would have never made it. I told him I was a spoiled rotten child of God. He said that was a great way to describe a life filled with the Lord. Well, I prayed for him and his situation before we got back to the dealership. My spare tire and the one I had brought from home was installed on my car, and I went home.

Later that evening, I was sharing my day with a friend and told him the story of my encounter with the young man. I told him how I said I was a spoiled rotten child of God, and suddenly, I felt a weight on top of me. All I could think to do was tell my friend about the pressure I felt and that I needed to go out on my front porch. He began to ask all kinds of questions about what was wrong, and all I could do was ask him to be quiet. The pressure didn't get any better out on the porch, and I told my friend I had to get out into the yard. He said he would call 911, and again, I requested silence.

Then I went out in my front yard under the stars. Suddenly, I could take a deep breath. I began to cry, and my friend said I was scaring him. I told him that God had just whispered to me that Spoiled Rotten Child of God was my new name. I will never forget that. I know it was a reminder to me of who I am and whose I am, and that I am a spoiled rotten child of God.

We are not supposed to cling tightly to our past in a way that holds us back or begins to define us, but in the hands of God, our past has purpose. When God reveals your purpose, He is setting you in motion. Back during my running years, the Lord sent me a word as I was in my own wilderness. He said, "Don't doubt in the darkness what was said to you in the light." Two phrases kept coming to my mind— "I know full well" and "in the fullness of time." These thoughts were followed by again looking to the Lord in prayer and to His Word to be reminded of what I know full well. These thoughts all gave me a hope that He had a plan for me that would come in the fullness of time.

Have you ever been asked to believe in a promise you can't see? God does seek your obedience to take a step in faith and motion to believe His promises. He loves nothing more than to see us move on the unseen.

I wish I had cried out to the Lord in the same way a father in Mark 9 did. He asked Jesus to heal his son who was possessed by demons. He said, "if you can." Jesus responded to that father by reminding him that "everything is possible for one who believes." Immediately, the boy's father said, "I do believe; help me overcome my unbelief!" (Mark 9:24). At this time, I was still having trouble believing about myself as much as God believed about me. So, He began to use the trials in my life to teach me who I wasn't so I could begin to believe who He says I am.

Since God had no plans to leave me or forsake me, I began to pray that He would take my biggest problems and issues to build my story in a way that it might be able to bring Him glory.

> Ephesians 1:7-12 speaks of God's plan for me. It says, *"In him we have redemption through his blood, the forgiveness of sins, in accordance with the riches of God's grace that he lavished on us. With all wisdom and understanding, he made known to us the mystery of his will according to his good pleasure, which he purposed in Christ, to be put into effect when the times reach their fulfillment—to bring unity to all things in heaven and on earth under Christ. In him we were also chosen, having been predestined according to the plan of him who works out everything in conformity with the purpose of his will, in order that we, who were the first to put our hope in Christ, might be for the praise of his glory."*

After Robert left, I experienced so many God moments in my life. I couldn't get enough of the fellowship I now had with the Lord in each moment of my days, and I was determined to saturate myself in God. I became so aware of His presence that I wanted nothing more than to be in that presence in any way possible. I plugged into the women's Bible study at Tuckaseege Baptist Church. We moved our meeting place to a multi-room house on the church grounds called the Life House. We met in the living room and dining room section of the house. The noise from the kids above us in the church building was a beautiful thing because it was an indication of church growth, but it was not very conducive to an atmosphere of intimacy where women could be real and raw. The Life House became a haven of prayer and encouragement.

I met there with a lot of women I already knew on a surface level and several who were new. That was also indicative of a growing church. We studied God's Word after we fellowshipped and shared our prayer requests. I believe the hearts that gather around prayer become knit together in a beautiful tapestry. I decided to take my story and share it with these ladies to possibly find a way to heal from the fallout of the past three years of my bad decisions.

I shared it from the perspective of the newfound love I had found in an intimate encounter with the Lord. I also shared how I laid myself at His feet looking for healing. I had gone from being covered in the dirt and grime of sin to giving Jesus my dirt to make into a healing clay for others. I told them the story of how I meditated on Psalm 139:23–24 after being led there as an answer to a devotional prayer. I also told them, God began to use this very scripture in me as I spoke it out loud to Him, and daily I began to lay my life at His feet as I talked to him.

I put the verses from Psalm 139 into a prayer in my own words— "Search me, God, and know my scared, hurt, broken, and mad heart. Test me in a way that I can learn from, and know all my thoughts, whether they be good, bad, or ugly. Let me know the ones that need healing, the ones that need rebuking and repenting of, and the ones that are just your child trying to come home. Lead me to filter these through Your loving hands. Amen."

I was coming to know God on a much deeper level, which I'm sure had a lot to do with trusting Him enough to lay all my faults at His feet for discussion and discipline. I came to a place of surrender that gave me a surprising feeling of complete freedom. It seems so directly opposite. But I had spent most of my life looking for a life partner who allowed me to be off duty. God was and is willing to give me peace and rest through the simple act of giving up my need to be in control.

I felt known and loved in the same way I felt when Michelle Chidester prayed over me in the tongues of the Holy Spirit. I realized I was surrounded in the love I had been looking for my whole life. I began to share Isaiah 43—what I called my life verses—with these women I was beginning to bond with in amazing ways every week. But now it meant more to me than the miracle of the scripture being presented to me as I drove down the highway. I was leaning on the words from Isaiah 43:1–3, 5 that assured me God was holding me right in His beautiful arms in all circumstances. It says,

> *"Do not fear, for I have redeemed you; I have summoned you by name; you are mine. When you pass through the waters, I will be with you; and when you pass through the rivers, they will not sweep over you. When you walk through the fire, you will not be burned; the flames will not set you ablaze. For I am the LORD your God, the Holy One of Israel, your Savior .... Do not be afraid, for I am with you."*

As I felt more confident, I also embraced Isaiah 43:18–19: "Forget the former things; do not dwell on the past. See, I am doing a new thing! Now it springs up; do you not perceive it? I am making a way in the wilderness and streams in the wasteland."

The world looked different. I could see more clearly, the sun was brighter, and colors were even more beautiful. To me, this is what hope looks like, *finally*! I found myself ministering to these women with my newfound hope. As I shared all the layers of my story, the women became more willing to be completely authentic in sharing their own stories and seeking the Lord for the help they needed. I started listening online to messages by Beth Moore, Priscilla Shirer, T. D. Jakes, and Bishop Jakes' daughter

Sarah Jakes Roberts and her husband Touré Roberts. They all fed me with their messages, but there are one or two that stood out to me in this stage of my life. Sarah's message "Girl, Get Up" inspired me to pick myself up and look for who I am in the Lord. But it was Touré's message "Abundance" that pointed me in the direction of my purpose and to believe it is possible that God's plan for my life was around before I was even thought of. In his message, he spoke of the echo of your life. 139:16–17 says, "Your eyes saw my unformed body; all the days were ordained for me written in your book before one of them came to be. How precious to me are your thoughts, God! How vast is the sum of them!"

My whole life has already happened in God's eyes. He has spoken every minute of my life into existence. The sound of God's voice is what I hear. I came to recognize the echo of my life when I started teaching a women's Bible study in my home. There was a beautiful confirmation in my spirit one night during one of those Bible study meetings. I realized that what I was doing felt completely natural as if I had been in this moment before. I described it as feeling like it was déja vu. It dawned on me that it was also a great way to describe walking in the echo of God's words over the moments of my life before any of them came to exist. I also had a confirmation in my spirit that this time in my life, from that day forward, was the culmination of a prophesy over my life 30 years earlier when I heard in my spirit that God wants to use my life to speak to women about Him.

I have always loved working in ministry, but now I know beyond a shadow of a doubt that my ministry focus is women. My life has been a real mess, but despite that God has used me, He has allowed me to experience beautiful miracles, and He has rescued me from not only circumstances but also from myself. I believe all of this points to His amazing grace and the extraordinary love He has bestowed on me, no matter what. That is exactly what I feel called to share with any woman who might say to me, "My life is too messed up for Jesus to love me or fix me" or "I will have to clean myself up before Jesus will accept me or save me." Neither of these is true.

I have always prayed that if I must go through the things I have gone through, please, Lord, let them help someone else. I also pray that the women the Lord puts into my care will be able to see through my story that God can redeem a broken, dysfunctional life and make it new. Hopefully, they will realize a time in their life when they, too, are walking in their echo. I believe that our deepest fear is not that we are inadequate. Our deepest fear is really that we are more powerful than we ever realize. We ask ourselves, who am I supposed to be? But we tend to paralyze ourselves by falling back to who am I not supposed to be.

We should allow ourselves to be brilliant, talented, and fabulous because we were born to make manifest the glory of God that is within us. And by letting our own light shine, we unconsciously give other people the permission to do the same.

I have learned that I am strong and outspoken, and some would say I have no filter. But if I am going to use these attributes to glorify God, I need to make sure I use the filter God gives me in his Word to correctly be strong and outspoken. I now know that I can stand on God's Word and His character as a GPS for my life—not as a restraint but to give me the accountability to be His servant. I pray that Jesus will be evident and manifested in my life in a way that points straight to the Lord. This is my responsibility if I am to walk in God's purpose for my life. I love the story of Isaiah's commission in Isaiah 6:1–8.

> *In the year that King Uzziah died, I saw the Lord, high and exalted, seated on a throne; and the train of his robe filled the temple. Above him were seraphim, each with six wings: With two wings they covered their faces, with two they covered their feet, and with two they were flying. And they were calling to one another: "Holy, holy, holy is the LORD Almighty; the whole earth is full of his glory." At the sound of their voices the doorposts*

and thresholds shook and the temple was filled with smoke. "Woe to me!" I cried. "I am ruined! For I am a man of unclean lips, and I live among a people of unclean lips, and my eyes have seen the King, the LORD Almighty." Then one of the seraphim flew to me with a live coal in his hand, which he had taken with tongs from the altar. With it he touched my mouth and said, "See, this has touched your lips; your guilt is taken away and your sin atoned for." Then I heard the voice of the Lord saying, "Whom shall I send? And who will go for us?" And I said, "Here am I. Send me!"

I asked God to cleanse my lips, my mind, and my heart to be worthy of His call on my life. And I continued praying Isaiah 139:23–24 over my life and listening for His voice and His direction.

One of the ministries I helped with at Tuckaseege Baptist Church was their monthly serving opportunities at Gastonia Street Ministries. As a group, we prepared a meal to feed 20 to 50 people. We served a meal, worshipped, and brought a message to the homeless and less fortunate. But truthfully, the blessings were also for us who served, and this night was no exception. I carpooled with another sister in Christ to the mission. I had gotten to know her through the Bible study I went to at the church. She was very much like me since she had not been raised with a silver spoon in her mouth, and we had lived some of the same journeys in life.

This night we were privileged to have our own Pastor Jason bring the message. His message was "The Story of the Lost Sheep" from Matthew 18:10–14. It tells of a shepherd who had 100 sheep. He loved all his sheep so much that if one, maybe only one, wandered off, that one was equally as important as the 99 who stayed close. He was willing to leave the 99 to go find the one that was lost. Under ordinary conditions, this story is always touching and speaks to how important we all are to God. But this night, my sister in Christ and I had a more expanded conversation about this parable on the way home. I am sure this was one of the days that was ordered and ordained for my life, and the Holy Spirit was right there in that car on the way home.

My friend and I talked about the times in our lives that we had strayed from the Lord and He had come looking for us because we were important to Him. The conversation went in a very raw direction, and I shared how I felt I had broken God's heart when I had an abortion at the age of 17. The car fell silent, and I could hear the sniffles, so I figured tears were coming from her in the seat beside me. She began to sob and said she had done the same thing, and this had been really burdening her. She continued to say that she had been praying for forgiveness for this and that she needed someone to talk to about this heartbreak in her life.

I managed to safely maneuver the car through my tears to drop her off at her home. We spoke of God's amazing grace and of the always on-time blessing of the Holy Spirit. This was the second time the Lord had answered my prayer to use my life in any and every way He saw fit to minister to another. And this wouldn't be the last. What both of us had done in our sin can remain a wound so deep that it is extremely hard to forgive yourself, not to mention believing that God can forgive you. But I will make myself available as God leads me to discover this secret among friends, church members, and even strangers so healing may occur. Again, I recognized that God has a distinctive plan for my life. Every time I experience being used by God for His purposes, I draw closer and closer to His heart and deeper and deeper in love with Him.

I believe we have an obligation to make ourselves prepared to walk in healthy ways through our purpose. So it is crucial that we give ourselves time in God's Word to stay full enough to give from a state of overflow, so our chances of depletion are less possible. Ephesians 2:10 says. "For we are God's handiwork, created in Christ Jesus to do good works, which God prepared in advance for us to do." I think that's a great way to relate to walking in our echo. Our good deeds were prepared in advance, we were known by God before we even existed, and all our days are written in His book before one came to be. Ephesians 2:10 also says that we were created in Christ Jesus. The best way to be in Christ Jesus is to know Him, and the best way to know Him is through His Word and surrendering to His will. Even though I am called by God, I still have some things that God is trying to work out on the inside of me.

Satan would have me believe that I am too damaged for God to use me. But God says to bring Him my damage and watch Him use it. I find comfort in believing that all my days were written in His book, and He knew where and how I got damaged. He must have considered that damage in the plans He has for my life. If I wait for everything in my world to be perfect, I will never operate in my purpose. So I have chosen to let this damage drive me to my destiny. If I don't allow God to transform the things that have been far, far from perfect in my life, I will transfer them onto everything moving forward. I can't allow my past to become my identity because 2 Corinthians 5:17 says, "If anyone is in Christ, the new creation has come. The old has gone, the new is here." There it is again—I am *in Christ*. So if I walk in Christ and in the dominion that God has given me, I will be unstoppable. Dominion in Christ is not control; it is territory.

My pastor, Michael Goins of Life Church in Cramerton, North Carolina, did a powerful sermon series about the table and its significance in the life of a believer. It was very life- changing for a people-pleaser like me. There was a part that spoke of knowing who is at your table, or your life. There are certain people you are not supposed to invite to your table, and that is by God's design. I used to be that person who tried to fix everybody and everything. But I have felt a great deal of freedom in learning how to say no, that I don't believe that is mine to do. It was very instrumental in learning how to stay in my lane.

I am far from perfect at this, but at least I can hear or receive the conviction of not practicing it. I have learned so much about just how important the Father, His Son, and His Holy Spirit are in my life. I used to hold on tightly to things and people, and I often gave away my dominion to them. In preparing to write this book, I went through years and years of journals. I gathered all the prayers that have wallpapered my prayer closet. I will tell you later how important I believe journaling and a prayer closet are.

This was one of the earlier prayer conversations I had with the Lord. "God, help me to yield to the cutting away of things that are dragging me down and stopping me from living in the joy of this beautiful life You have given me. I am ready to let go of things that can be shaken away from me in my life. And show me that these are the things that will never be devoted to me and that get in the way of my devotion to You. You are my only constant. May I give my devotion totally to You."

I like to say that I live my life for an audience of One. I think it is so awesome that the audience I live my life for now loves me and has only His best in mind for me. I have heard so many people ask God to show them their purpose, and I believe our ultimate purpose in life is to glorify God. If we are always doing, saying, and preparing our thoughts on ways to glorify God, everything that falls in line with that will be beautiful and fill your soul to overflowing. Once I realized what I was supposed to use in and from my life to bring glory to God, I got an unquenchable yearning to operate for that purpose.

To feel at home in what I know to be my gift is wonderful, but I never want to miss God's vision for my purpose. There are so many more blessings on this journey with Jesus. I have realized that my strength has increased as I follow step by step with Christ. He has taken me from strength to strength and glory to glory. According to Romans 12:2, I plan not to be conformed to the pattern of this world but to be transformed by the renewing of my mind. Then I will be able to test and approve what God's will is—His good, pleasing, and perfect will.

Chapter 15

The Helper That Fellowships, Frees, and Heals

Romans 5:5 says, "And hope does not put us to shame, because God's love has been poured out into our hearts through the Holy Spirit, who has been given to us." The Holy Spirit funnels the love of God and Jesus to us, so we feel them with us in their absence. Before Jesus was crucified, buried, and rose from the dead, He tried to comfort His disciples about His not being there in the future. He told them in the 14th chapter of John that He would ask the Father to send an advocate to help them who would be with them forever as the Spirit of Truth.

I like to use the pronoun *He* for the Spirit of Truth because He is a person to me—my friend, my guide, and my partner. We are tight. This chapter, especially this part about the Holy Spirit, will have a lot of scripture because I don't know how else to honor my friend when I talk about Him. In John 16, after the crucifixion and resurrection and shortly before Jesus's ascension to heaven, He spoke to his disciples and told them what to expect after He goes away. They had a lot of anxiety about not having Jesus lead them through the continuation of His ministry. He tells them how they will be ostracized and persecuted as they try to move on in His ministry. He feels their fear but tells them this in John 16:4–7:

> *I have told you this, so that when their time comes you will remember that I warned you about them. I did not tell you this from the beginning because I was with you, but now I am going to him who sent me. None of you asks me, "Where are you going?" Rather, you are filled with grief because I have said these things. But very truly I tell you, it is for your good that I am going away. Unless I go away, the Advocate will not come to you; but if I go, I will send him to you.*

I love that Jesus uses the pronoun *he* when speaking of the Holy Spirit. My friend, the Holy Spirit, has been involved in many ways throughout my life. I believe the first time I was introduced to Him was the time I have already spoken of when I was driving down the highway to work and heard "Isaiah 43" in my spirit. I found a Bible to read the encouragement I needed for that day and time in my life. I was told in that scripture that I was called by name, and He calls me His.

This happened shortly after I had my bathroom floor time of my salvation, which I have also spoken of. At that time, along with the forgiveness of my sins, I was given the same Advocate that Jesus told the disciples about who would come to be with them to guide them through life and ministry. This Advocate would be with me all through my life. Ephesians 1:13–14 says, "And you also were included in Christ when you heard the message of truth, the gospel of your salvation. When you believed, you were marked in him with a seal, the promised Holy Spirit, who is a deposit guaranteeing our inheritance until the redemption of those who are God's possession—to the praise of his glory."

The biblical use of the word *advocate* is to describe someone who pleads another's cause or defends or comforts. In the Greek, the word for advocate is *parakletos*, which means "helper, advisor, or counselor." That pretty much says what the Spirit of God is to me. One Sunday while I was standing for praise and worship at the Nazarene church, I was deep in confusion and depression. I know beyond a shadow of a doubt that I heard the Holy Spirit speak and say, "No matter what." It was exactly what I needed to hear to assure me that I could get through what I was going through or anything that came my way because I have God and Jesus with me through the Holy Spirit.

About the same time, I was in a Bible study that profoundly spoke to me through Exodus 14:14, which says, "The Lord will fight for you; you need only to be still." Moses spoke these words to the Israelites to assure them right after crossing the Red Sea that they would never again see the Egyptians who were chasing them because God was doing all the fighting for them to get away. Moses was telling them there was nothing for them to do but trust and be still.

In many preceding chapters, I have told you that I know I have heard the Spirit speak. For example, it happened the night it was confirmed that the name I prayed for God to give me was Spoiled Rotten Child of God. And I know when I was covered in a feeling of heaviness on my body, the covering of the Holy Spirit was so heavy that I couldn't breathe until I got outside under the stars with the Lord to share that moment. I also know that it was the Holy Spirit speaking through me in the plan of God when I got to minister to three other women who have carried the guilt of abortion in their life, just like me. And in the last two years, I have been filled differently with the Spirit, and I can pray in tongues in a way that overwhelms my normal speech to converse with God in an intimate way that shares His thoughts. Even now, I struggle to use adequate words to describe this beautiful experience.

I also believe it is my partnership with the Holy Spirit that is helping me learn to feel an agitation of my soul when I encounter spirits in my world that are up to nothing but tearing me or my environment apart. When we are being seduced by the evil one, the Holy Spirit will say, "No, no, no." Walking in the Holy Spirit will give us a discernment that if something feels off, it probably is. The same Holy Spirit that was there when Christ was raised from the dead lives in me, thank goodness. He has taken hold of me and my thoughts and behaviors when I am willing to listen and has freed me from the ones that would have bound me in ways that only tear me down.

By being led into more healthy thinking, I have been delivered from myself and my own stinkin' thinkin.' The Holy Spirit also guides me in those gray areas where I am not entirely sure what to do, or when I am completely deceived and played by this world. He is so loving to remind me that I should only consider what God thinks of me and look away from the negative definitions of me that come from others. Second Timothy 3 tells us to search our heart through God's Word and the Holy Spirit. The Holy Spirit will never instruct us in any way that is contrary to God's Word.

I do so much better when I listen to the Holy Spirit because He has a way to bring up convictions in my heart about my behavior, but He also warns me and gives me an uneasiness to guide me away from worldly deceit. I have to say that I am not perfect at always realizing His guidance, but I am better at it than I used to be, and I seek growth in that area for my life. But what I regularly rely on is the fact that if I just ask, the Holy Spirit will intercede for me when I don't know what to pray in any circumstance.

First Corinthians 2:12–14 tells us that the spirit of human wisdom, or the wisdom of this age, is alienated from God because of the attitude of the sinful nature. Many fail to understand true wisdom because such wisdom is spiritual in the mature Christian. A person without the Holy Spirit perceives things from mere instinct or opinion, based on physical, worldly, or natural life. Spiritual wisdom is gained with the dwelling of the Holy Spirit, which comes with the new birth through salvation. I hope and pray that I continue to grow and learn from my partnership with the Holy Spirit. It has changed many of my old ways to the more productive ways in which I now move in my world.

I am so thankful that God gave me the Holy Spirit to teach me, protect me, and motivate me in growth as a Christian who hopefully glorifies Him. I believe that God has expectations written all over His Word, and they ultimately are for our good and can lead to easier, happier, healthier living. I have personally seen the Holy Spirit help me get to the place where I can forgive people for very deep hurts in my life. He has also led me to the place where I am willing to come to the truth of what I need to ask forgiveness for, especially the sins I have perpetuated against my beloved Lord. And those experiences have brought healing to my body and my soul.

I believe it is human tendency to talk to our friends first about how we have sinned. I'm not sure if this is because we are seeking these people to absolve us in some sort of way or to love on us and tell us, "Oh, God knows your heart, and He knows you didn't mean to do it." We can also take it to someone we lean on for counseling. Having trusted friends and counsel is always good, but just talking to people about our sins will not bring us forgiveness or release us from guilt or responsibility. Talking to people is like putting Scotch tape on a hemorrhaging wound of secrets.

I learned about a prayer closet from a movie Priscilla Shirer starred in. In the movie, she was mentored by an older woman she came to know who taught her how to take all her secret thoughts, attitudes, problems, and unconfessed sin to the Lord in prayer. She showed Priscilla her room that was completely dedicated to her prayer time and fellowship with the Lord. Priscilla gave it a try, and a funny thing happened. God began to change Priscilla, and because she committed to her prayer time with the Lord, He honored that as He moved in the circumstances in her life. I have such a room, or closet, where I am spending a lot of prayer time or time in general. Sometimes I pray, sometimes I read my Bible, sometimes I study, and sometimes I just go in there to listen and rest in the arms of my Father. I want to encourage you to find a space where you can be alone with the Lord, rest in the arms of Jesus, and listen to the Holy Spirit. It is like a clubhouse for you and your three best friends. You can solve a lot of problems in there.

Do you know that hiding the truth of your sin is a design of the devil? It is so harmful that your body, mind, and heart are influenced by it. Pain in your body can be a symptom of truth that is unexpressed or that you haven't brought to the light of God's mercy, grace, and forgiveness. Our bodies weren't meant to carry the burden of unconfessed hurts and lies. It shows up in the way you talk to people and how you relate to them. Love can be tainted by running it through these unexpressed hurts and lies. God is the only One who can forgive us and eradicate our sins in a way that will heal us and set us free. His mercy comes through the love that held Jesus on the cross where He bled and died for our sins. We just need to skip the middleman and take sinful secrets straight to God.

Satan wants us to stop short of what the cross offers us. He wants to use our secrets that we don't confess and repent of to control us and separate us from God. In the same manner, if we refuse to forgive those who have wronged us, we will separate ourselves from God and compromise the measure of forgiveness we will get from God. Jesus said in Mark 11:25 that if we forgive people when they sin against us, our heavenly Father will also forgive us. If we don't forgive people for their sins, our heavenly Father will not forgive us.

Not forgiving someone who hurt you can resemble a seriously deep infection that only gets worse with time. It will separate you from God, but that unforgiveness truly can also affect your health. It has been said that unforgiveness is like drinking poison and expecting someone else to die. Those who are holding onto unforgiveness don't realize that the unforgiveness is controlling them as much or more than the original hurt. Forgiveness should be motivated by how much we have been forgiven, and Jesus doesn't ask us to give any more or less than He has given us.

In Ephesians 4:31–32, Paul wrote, "Get rid of all bitterness, rage, and anger, brawling and slander, along with every form of malice. Be kind and compassionate to one another, forgiving each other, just as in Christ God forgave you." Recently I heard these thoughts on my favorite Christian radio station near my home. The morning show hosts shared this: "When I fail to forgive, I exaggerate the offense toward me, and I minimize my offense against God." Sometimes the most courageous thing we can do is forgive.

In the case of Joseph in Genesis 47, he chose to use his position after being betrayed by his brothers to help them and all their clan survive a famine that crippled all of Egypt and Canaan. His older brothers came to him for help, not knowing who he was. But he knew who they were and had no malice toward them. He helped them because he recognized that his life after betrayal was now being used by God for good. If he had not forgiven his brothers, it could have been a wedge between him and God, who called him to be the one who saved a nation.

Forgiveness has not always been easy for me. I used to think that a price had to be paid for forgiveness. I was even so arrogant that I called myself "the queen of accountability" in a way that I always owned up to everything I did, and so should everyone else. But I don't remember including much about asking for forgiveness for what I had done. But praise God that the Holy Spirit worked His love on me and showed me that my accountability was not worth a thing if it wasn't followed by humility and a contrite heart, asking for forgiveness.

Once again on the flip side, it is only through a willingness to forgive an offense that I could find a freedom and healing that has changed my life.

I can't tell you how many times God's healing hand has saved me from near death. But wait. I have done that several times already in my story. I don't want to miss telling you about a couple more instances that I have been saved from and brought to healing to be kept for God's purposes. Here are a few.

I have had an upset stomach that made me so sick that I couldn't hold anything down for almost a week. After I was misdiagnosed at the ER, I finally made it into a triage appointment with my family doctor's physician's assistant and found out I had an amoebic infection in my stomach from unwashed fresh vegetables at a restaurant. It turns out that I was 24 hours away from intensive care at the hospital.

In a similar fashion, I was bitten by a brown recluse spider. I tried to treat the bite like any other bug bite. It turned into flesh-eating bacteria. Again, if the doctor I finally saw hadn't debrided the infection and treated me with high dose antibiotics, I could have died. While all of this is truly scary to think about now, I am truly blessed that my God intervened on my behalf.

These don't even compare to the feeling of getting a spiritual healing. In Psalm 103:1–5, David wrote, "Praise the Lord, my soul; all my inmost being, praise his holy name. Praise the Lord, my soul, and forget not all his benefits—who forgives all your sins and heals all your diseases, who redeems your life from the pit and crowns you with love and compassion, who satisfies your desires with good things so that your youth is renewed like the eagle's." The Lord works righteousness and justice for all the oppressed. But if we don't have the relationship with the Lord that draws us to the Him when we are facing trials or suffering, I do believe that Satan can work on us in a way to make us doubt ourselves. But if we sign on for the self-doubt for long enough, it can begin to defeat us and become such a stronghold that it sets us up to be a target for Satan to attack us.

People unfortunately can also be used as Satan's minions in a way to try to keep us under that thumb of oppression where our past once kept us. We don't have to stay in our past or remain the victim of another's disrespect. But if we don't continue to reclaim the territory the Lord is providing us in the land of healing and wholeness, reprogram our minds to think of ourselves as a child of the King, and see ourselves through His eyes, we may slip right back into the lies we once believed. You can't just drive out the bad spirits; you must refill your heart, mind, and soul with the Holy Spirit in such a way that there's no room for you to get triggered by your past.

Dealing with your past in the healthy way that God intended is exactly opposite of what Satan would have you do. You don't have to live as trampled ground, as a life with painful thorns of misery, and with thoughts that bring forth no fruitfulness, no strength, and keep you defeated and fearful. We should operate out of the fullness of who we are in Christ, trade in our old operating systems, and be healed.

I believe it is with the partnership I have with the Holy Spirit that I am learning to feel an agitation of my soul when I encounter spirits in my life that plan to try to tear me down and rock my whole environment. When we are being seduced by the evil one, the Holy Spirit will be saying no. We can receive discernment from Him. If we are walking with Him and listening, we will realize that if something feels off, it probably is. Second Timothy 1:7 (NKJV) says, "God hasn't given us a spirit of fear, but of power and of love and of a sound mind." We have the right in Christ to be a whole, healthy, happy person. We can trust that we belong to the One who will never leave us or forsake us.

I have two rescue Beagles. The first one I brought home is named Ginger. She is a beautiful mini–Chocolate Beagle. She was someone's breed dog. When she came to live with her foster mom Jennifer, she didn't know what grass was. We suspected that she was kept in some kind of kennel or a shed with a concrete floor. We guessed that she had been neglected, abused, and abandoned until she was needed for her service. She did not know how to love because of how she was conditioned by her environment. She did not know what to do when I held her and loved on her, and she was scared of everything. I decided after a month of her being shy and scared to death that she might need a friend, so I rescued a sister for her. I named her sister Sunshine, or Sunny for short. Sunny was very happy to be free from her life in a kennel for eight to 12 hours a day. She loves her mommy (me), Ginger, all people, and attention. Sunny has helped Ginger come out of her fear and doubt that was instilled in her. She learned what pure love feels like.

Sunny learned what freedom and attention look like. She also is living her best delayed puppy life, and I might say that it was at the expense of many things that were shredded by the time I got home. My two sweet Beagle girls have taught me much about myself too. I learned so much from watching them come out of their past lives and begin to trust me and know that I love them dearly and will never leave them.

Ginger and Sunny had to reprogram their beliefs and build new memories of trust to begin to live their best lives, as I have. I have struggled with breaking free from self-defeating thoughts, and to this day there are times when Satan or the people he can use do their best to try to remind me of who I used to be. My own healing is very similar to Ginger and Sunny's in that I had to overcome my past by allowing, receiving, and believing that I have been healed by God spiritually through His love, the sacrifices of Jesus on my behalf, and the fellowship I have had with the Holy Spirit.

I can't finish this chapter about healing without speaking about Satan's use of spirits that he can deploy to draw us back into captivity. We should be aware that we can be made sick when we get covered in the control of a demonic spirit. I believe I took one with me from the Nazarene church, the site of the collapse of my first marriage. That spirit of evil and manipulation that controlled my husband had a friend that I believe attached itself to me and manifested itself in what John Bevere talks about in his book *The Bait of Satan* as a spirit of offense. My pastor gave me this book as a tool that might help me.

I recognized that I may be covered by this very spirit of offense. And it is exactly like it sounds. It manipulates your mind in such a way that you are just waiting for the ill feelings that you perceive are being directed at you. The spirit of offense was what Satan was trying to use to keep me bound to the defeating talk in my head and try to insert back into my life the feeling of not being worthy of the call I know is on my life. I had to loudly and verbally rebuke that spirit of offense off me before it settled in. I knew better than to let it get a hold of me or twist innocent words into something they weren't. I couldn't let hurt feelings take root or let myself feel defeated over something that was never meant to wound me in the first place. It was so freeing not to have all my relationships filtered through expecting everyone in my life to have a negative opinion of me.

I do remember the time of being disrespected and treated as if I was lesser than, but it was only through finally rebuking of that spirit and being determined to live my life for an audience of one, that I was finally delivered from always being ready for a fight. My advice for anyone who feels the way I did is to not leave the door open to Satan's accusations that make you feel not good enough or that you are crazy. Let your ears and your spirit hear nothing less than what God says about you.

All our experiences can become something we can use to glorify God or help someone we may encounter who is going through the same sort of things we have experienced. Several years ago, I told the Lord to use my history to build a testimony that was honoring of Him. But I harbored all kinds of pain and dysfunction from the feelings of neglect I felt from the way my mother raised me. After reading a portion of a book that was about a woman whose mother had hurt her badly in her childhood, but she finally got the apology she had sought for years, I started to cry. I told the Lord how much I wanted that from my mom. The Holy Spirit asked me if I really wanted my mother at age 90 to relive the pain she had caused me and for her to ask for my forgiveness. The Lord said, "Let me have all that pain, disappointment, and resentment, and you never have to carry it again." I was so relieved to be free of the resentment and the unforgiveness that had kept me bound for most of my life.

I like to think of my life like newfound gold. When newfound gold is put in fire, it melts away the impurities, called the dross, which is scooped away to reveal the purest of gold that shines in the most spectacular ways. Pain is sometimes providential in God's plan. The pain that God works through leads to growth and will never disappoint. It can reveal beautiful things in your life. And that day I was free from all that had held me back and was purified of all the dross in my life, and I was like the purest of gold.

First Peter 5:10 says, "And the God of all grace, who called you to his eternal glory in Christ, after you have suffered a little while, will himself restore you and make you strong, firm and steadfast." If you believe and count on the fact that God has a plan in all things, then the best thing to do in a crisis is to give yourself a moment, but only a moment, before you seek God's will on how to move forward. Don't starve yourself of the blessing in the healing. And lean into the healing and the strength the indwelling of the Holy Spirit gives you. Recognize God using that strength to move you forward. Let this be a day of awakening to see the healing power of God. Ask God to open your eyes to the victory and freedom found in complete surrender.

Chapter 16

Using Your Failures, Faith, Fellowship, and Even Your Face for Ministry

D o you wonder if you are called to ministry? Are you absolutely sure that is what you were made for? I know certain things about myself. I have a big mouth, and I love to talk. But I also know that I love people, most of the time. But there is one thing I unequivocally know, and that is that I love God with all my heart and want to live out the rest of my days telling the world how much God loves me and how much he loves the people He trusts me with in ministry.

I heard God speak through the Holy Spirit into my life over 30 years ago. I heard in my spirit the voice of God telling me that I will speak to many, many people in my life about Him. I did not know at the time what that meant. But I have over the years learned that anywhere can become a mission field for you to serve in. I have had the distinct responsibility to be the crossing guard at the elementary school and the middle school in my little town of Mount Holly. I never really thought I was some extreme kid person, but I get lots of tiny hugs because apparently the kids think I am. It is my honor to let all those little people know that they are loved by me and, when I get a chance, I tell them, that they are loved by God too.

Along with the children, I also take it very seriously to care about the parents. It wasn't easy raising kids when I was a young parent, but it is even more challenging these days. In the two years that I have had my precious job, I have gotten to know many of the families. I have seen family expansion and deaths of cherished loved ones. I have seen how teenage rebellion can tear apart a family. But one of the things I have witnessed from these parents is the morning mad faces I see when they drive by me, after they have pleaded and begged their kids to eat their breakfast, brush their teeth, actually wear two of the same shoes, and hurry, hurry, hurry to get in the car. I have made it my responsibility, even if the kids have already been dropped off, to make these frazzled people have a good laugh when they flash their lights and honk their horn at me, to which I respond with my version of some kind of waving dance. I try to wipe off the mad faces and bring on a smile as they pass this crazy waving person on their way to work. I have even made others like a motorcycle officer from Charlotte honk and smile as she goes down the two- lane highway parallel to my location. I am so thankful that God has found a place of service for my less-than-perfect face to be used to love on these kids and their parents.

I have heard so many people over the years ask the same cryptic question: I have spoken of in prior pages, and that is "God, please tell me what the purpose of my life is." To that I say again that the bottom-line purpose of your life is to *glorify God*. If you do that, you will be loving God in such an intimate way that He will show you a place you can come alongside of Him, where He is already working. In the meantime, know the first commandment, and love God and love your neighbor as yourself. Then, when or if you are called into ministry, your heart is already primed for any assignment.

I have heard a story told by many pastors in my lifetime that describes a young man who is very serious about ministry who comes to his pastor one day and says, "Pastor, can I meet with you tomorrow so you can teach me what I need to know about being a pastor? I believe I am ready." The next day the young man showed up to the pastor's office, and the first thing the pastor told him to do was look in the janitor's closet, get out the toilet brush, and go clean the bathrooms. The young man said to the pastor, "But Pastor, I came here to learn what I need to do to be a pastor, not to clean toilets." The pastor said, "Well, son, the first thing you need to learn to be a pastor and serve the Lord is humility." If I could add to that I would have sent the young man to a nursing home to feed an elderly person who can no longer feed themselves. I believe that an equally important attribute to being in ministry is love. If we desire to be in ministry, we need to have the two most profound characteristics of Jesus—humility and love.

Pastor Jason Marlowe has said quite often that we are to love God completely, ourselves correctly, and others compassionately. Pastor Michael Todd of Transformation Church preached a message about what a calling to ministry looks like. He said in true ministry, you could be serving in a number of capacities. Those places might be behind the scenes, but you are still working for the glory of God. He presented an example with some of his staff on stage with him and instructed them to follow him wherever he went on that stage. They were all positioned behind him. He walked three steps up, and so did his staff. He moved four steps to the right, and so did his staff. He told them to fall in behind him in a line, and they did. And then he took one step back. He then asked the congregation if they could see the guy who was right behind him, and they shouted *no*. His illustration was that to be in ministry with the Lord, we have to do as we are told, but we also must be ready to follow. But the most important thing we need to be ready to do is to be right behind the Lord in ministry, even if we are not seen. Then the pastor expanded his thought to say that the guy behind him was so close to him, that even though he couldn't be seen, and was maybe in his shadow, he was close enough to hear him breathing.

I'm here to say that I would be humbled and blessed to serve in ministry with Jesus even if I am unseen in His shadow. That would indicate just how close I am to Him—close enough to hear Him breathing. What a profound privilege that would be.

I once was scolded about how I told my testimony, and that didn't sit well with me. I tried to take it as constructive criticism, and then the person elaborated. He told me that I was acting way too arrogant in my delivery, and I needed to start trying to be more aware of how many times I said I, me, and my. Well, I stewed over that, and it didn't take long before I said I don't know how to share my testimony without using I, me, or my because (I) have lived a filthy dirty life, but Jesus saved (me) in spite of myself, and (I) know that (my) God loves me so much that He died for (me), and (I) know that (my) life will never be the same.

We are supposed to try to be humble in ministry and in life, but C. S. Lewis said, "Humility is not thinking less of yourself, it's thinking of yourself less." I believe that we can't teach what we don't know, so (I) am telling (my) story.

To be humble in ministry is never done by putting ourselves down, because by doing that, we diminish the God who called us. As a matter of fact, it took me a long time to embrace that prophecy over my life about speaking to many about God because I was so enslaved to every label that anyone had put on me in my life. I thought that to keep the peace I had to accept all the derogatory comments that were pronounced over my life. That behavior was birthed all the way back in my childhood when I felt unseen and not good enough.

If you are a people pleaser like I was my whole life, you probably do not know who your authentic self really is. You are too busy living up to whomever has an expectation of who you should be or how you should act. There are many things that happen by trying to be the creation or design of anyone other than God. Sometimes we create these unrealistic standards of who we should be. Sometimes it's life that sets up scenarios that we fall into and lose ourselves in while trying to live up to a worldly standard. I tried so hard to be perfect, or at least as close as I could get to perfect. That caused me to be devoted to good things that were a measuring stick for just how perfect I was aiming to be. I loved all these things deeply. They were my husband, my kids, my friends, and my work. They deserved my perfection, and apparently, some of them seemed to think they could demand it too. When I failed at anything, or even fell short, I fell off the pedestal I felt I had to stay perched on. It was exhausting. All these things became idols to me because I was living my life trying not to disappoint anyone. I made all my relationships more important to me than my relationship with God.

When God says that we are not to let anything come before him, these words are not aimed at the things, or people that we make our idols. They are aimed at us when we allow anything to surpass His importance in our lives. My Egypt and my land of slavery—of my own making, I should say—was what took precedence in my life. The things I idolized were all things I loved, but they were never supposed to come before God. It is God who meant for me to not be in slavery to anything or anybody, to put Him first, and to put my relationship with Him on the top of my list so I could serve Him. Having anything or anybody that takes more of your heart, mind, and soul than God may impeach a call to ministry. There were the seasons after my divorce when I was living anything but a holy life fit for His service. Again, the brokenness that still haunted me kept me searching for a place or a person who I mattered to.

Living that life that was willing to compromise anything and everything just to not be alone is no life that God will use to glorify him. So I pushed the call farther and farther away by the immoral dating, the unforgiveness in my heart, the uncontrollable anger, manipulation, the need for control, the living with Al and Robert before marriage which was never in God's plan. I still remembered that prophecy over my life in the back of my mind, and I secretly had the desire for ministry. But that door was shut because of my lifestyle. I wanted to be a witness for the Lord, but who would believe me? In all the negative attributes that I was labeled with, the one that broke my heart the most was made real to me through hearing two completely different women tell me that God has a plan for your life but He's not going to reveal it to you as long as you're living your life the way you are.

As many critics as I have had in my life, there is one voice I can't shake—*mine*. I had to get to a place where I could believe what God was saying about me, so that others could believe what I was saying about God. I am slowly coming to believe that by taking hold of who I am in Christ and who I have been called to be, I give those who come behind me the permission to do the same. That is my prayer for the mission of this book.

That she who reads this will believe Luke 1:45, which I planted in my own spirit. It says, "Blessed is she who has believed that the Lord would fulfill his promises to her."

Exodus 3 and 4 is a depiction of Moses's conversation with God in the desert through a burning bush that was not being burned up in the fire. Moses argued with God who told him He was going to use him to lead the Israelites out of Egypt. Moses makes all kinds of excuses, probably because it is said that Moses had a speech impediment. God got angry with Moses for resisting the call and ultimately doubting Him. This is one of the few times in Scripture where God gets angry. God assures Moses that He will send his brother Aaron with him to get the job done. And then later in the story, Moses writes this in Deuteronomy 32:1–4:

> *Listen, you heavens, and I will speak; hear, you earth, the words of my mouth. Let my teaching fall like rain and my words descend like dew, like showers on new grass, like abundant rain on tender plants. I will proclaim the name of the LORD. Oh, praise the greatness of our God! He is the Rock, his works are perfect, and all his ways are just. A faithful God who does no wrong, upright and just is he.*

What beautiful words Moses taught his people, to glorify God in the face of their rebellion. And even though he was not to enter the Promised Land, God gave Moses this glorified speech as he was breathing the air of his last days.

Gideon also disagreed with the angel of the Lord who called Gideon a "mighty man of valor" when he was hiding from the Midianites while he was threshing wheat in a winepress. And as with Moses, God showed up to help Gideon carry out the delivery of the Israelites from the hands of the Midianites. These men doubted God's call on their lives, and it was only when they took steps toward moving in what God was calling them to do that God elevated them and showed up to help.

I believe God speaks to us in a way that we understand. His loving voice wants to have a conversation with the person He made us to be. He will not speak to the faux you. It is that person He wants to send out to speak for Him that he will converse with. He already knows who you really are and who He is sending you to. He has made no plans for that faux you. That's why it is so important that you be the authentic you. The ones He sends you to aren't looking for the faux you.

I believe there is a sound your life has made since the day you were born. But in the supernatural, that sound is the voice of God calling you to your existence. It is the sound of God ordaining your steps. In Jeremiah 1:5, the

Lord said through Jeremiah, "Before I formed you in the womb I knew you, before you were born, I set you apart; I appointed you as a prophet to the nations." I pray that these words speak of my life as well.

When I realized that my purpose is in women's ministry, I saw what walking in my echo felt like. I figured out why ministering to women like me always feels like I am living in a huge déja vu. The reason I feel like I have already been there and done that is because all my days are already recorded for me in the book of life. I was created by God to play the one who has or is living the story He has already written for me.

It is in believing that God wants the best for me and is equipping me for the call on my life that I can become the vessel He wants me to be. I am learning to walk in the honor of His calling, and I must be strong in my convictions because He's not going to send somebody wishy-washy or somebody who doesn't have confidence in what they are conveying. He has called me, and I need to say, "Speak, Lord, your servant is listening."

Proverbs 3:5–6 says, "Trust in the LORD with all your heart and lean not on your own understanding; in all your ways submit to him, and he will make your paths straight." This is so true, and I pray that any of my sweet sisters who read this story of how God redeemed my life just for Him will yearn to do their best to discover their own echo.

I want to leave with you one of the best scriptures I know for self-discovery. David, the man after God's own heart, wrote this in Psalm 139:1–24:

You have searched me, LORD, and you know me. You know when I sit and when I rise; you perceive my thoughts from afar. You discern my going out and my lying down; you are familiar with all my ways. Before a word is on my tongue you, LORD, know it completely. You hem me in behind and before, and you lay your hand upon me. Such knowledge is too wonderful for me, too lofty for me to attain. Where can I go from your Spirit? Where can I flee from your presence? If I go up to the heavens, you are there; if I make my bed in the depths, you are there. If I rise on the wings of the dawn, if I settle on the far side of the sea, even there your hand will guide me, your right hand will hold me fast. If I say, "Surely the darkness will hide me and the light become night around me," even the darkness will not be dark to you; the night will shine like the day, for darkness is as light to you. For you created my inmost being; you knit me together in my mother's womb. I praise you because I am fearfully and wonderfully made; your works are wonderful, I know that full well. My frame was not hidden from you when I was made in the secret place, when I was woven together in the depths of the earth. Your eyes saw my unformed body; all the days ordained for me were written in your book before one of them came to be. How precious to me are your thoughts, God! How vast is the sum of them! Were I to count them, they would outnumber the grains of sand—when I awake, I am still with you. If only you, God, would slay the wicked! Away from me, you who are bloodthirsty! They speak of you with evil intent; your adversaries misuse your name. Do I not hate those who hate you, Lord, and abhor those who are in rebellion against you? I have nothing but hatred for them; I count them my enemies. Search me, God, and know my heart; test me and know my anxious thoughts. See if there is any offensive way in me and lead me in the way everlasting.

In Closing

In the pages of this book, some would say I told the story of my life. But to me, I feel incredibly humbled to have been called to the privilege of talking about my broken life and defiled testimony for the purpose of glorifying God and how His mercy and grace redeemed my life and my testimony into His service. I am so blessed to have the privilege of doing this. I know the Lord has saved me and protected me to finish this journey to honor Him.

I have already spoken on the previous pages about how God kept me through several near-death experiences and other times that could have caused trouble for me and ruined my life. I have been healed more than once in His keeping of me. I have shared stories of unexplained phenomena like the word Hope in the sky and the covering by the Spirit at the revealing of my God-given name. I have written about the whisper of Isaiah 43 into my heart on my way to work. But there are a couple of other things I want to leave you with. I had a 100-year-old maple tree in my front yard back in 2018, and I began to notice that the limbs were starting to get closer and closer to the ground. I asked a tree trimming company to come and check it out. Upon examination, they determined that the tree was sick and needed to come down. The tree company quoted me $3,600 to remove it. I was in a panic because I did not have that kind of money lying around. I spoke to my pastor at the time, Jason Marlowe from Tuckaseege Baptist Church, about a benevolence that may be available for some financial help to get that tree taken down. He told me he would confer with the deacons and get back to me about how the church might be able to help me.

At that time and even now, I am in the habit of journaling. In my journal entries, I just talk to God in a conversation or a prayer about my life. There is an entry in my journal on July 3, 2018, that says, "Please, God, can you show me how to get this tree taken out of my yard, and in the meantime, will you please keep me and my Beagle dog Dixie safe?" I still have that journal, and I have a picture of that entry on my phone because I never want to forget it. Right after I wrote that, Pastor Jason called to tell me that the deacons would meet that morning, and he would have an answer for me. I told him that I didn't understand why, but I had complete peace about the whole situation.

After that phone call, I heard in my spirit, "Prepare." And without questioning, I took Dixie's leash out to the fence beside my house, and I called my neighbors and told them to keep their kids out from under the tree because it is getting worse. If anything happened to the tree, I asked them to please get Dixie out of the house. With that being taken care of, I went on about my business, got dressed, and went to work around the corner. Three hours later, I got a call from my neighbor that the tree had fallen on my house. My house was covered by the tree, but they had managed to get Dixie out safely. There's a lot more to the story, but I have pictures of the time my house, my dog, and I were all kept by God's intervention.

I also have a story about what should have been a devastating traffic accident near my house on June 30, 2023. On that day at about 5:00 p.m., I was three blocks from home when I entered an intersection after going through the green light, only to have a car blow through a red light and crash into my car. The driver was on a T-bone collision course for my car, but when she hit me, all the damage was to the front of my car. There is video footage of the crash from the corner gas station, and you can see her headed right for the side of my car. The police were so sure that she would have hit me in the side of my car so hard, that they kept asking me if I had been flipped over. I give thanks to God that He had kept me again. I did spend about 18 hours in a trauma unit, but I made a complete recovery.

I will wrap this up with one last story. I saved the best for last. It depends on how you look at this, but I see it as an example of the scriptures that I have spoken about in the story that mentioned God predestines your life even before you are born. A few years ago, I started having some balance and pain issues that sent me to a neurologist to see if I had multiple sclerosis. I had an MRI, and the neurologist referred me to a neurosurgeon for further study. I received word from the neurosurgeon that he wanted to take my MRI to a national brain tumor conference to confer with his peers about what the MRI showed. Talk about scaring someone almost to death! He was out of town for weeks, and when he came back, he finally shared that I have what's called a cephalocele on my brain. I could have had it since birth, and usually children have complications from this deformity that can kill them or cause them to be institutionalized. Then he said, "There's more, but it is good news." Well, I needed some kind of redemption for what I thought was pretty bad news. He told me, "You have a malformation of your skull, but the cephalocele is tucked inside that malformation so it has not been allowed to grow as it usually would."

I have a picture of that on my MRI, but better than that I have a sincere and documented reason that I will praise the Lord with my whole life. In Ephesians 3:20–21, Paul may have felt like me when he wrote, "Now to him who is able to do immeasurably more than all we ask or imagine, according to his power that is at work within us, to him be glory in the church and in Jesus Christ throughout all generations, forever and ever! Amen."

Special Thanks

Thank the Lord for trusting me to share my story to Glorify Him.

I also want to thank all the people in my life who did not give up on me, stood by me, and believed in me in spite of myself.

A special thanks to my photographer, Kayla Orellana, who made me feel beautiful.

And finally, thank you, thank you, thank you, to my team at Lucid. I love y'all!